MW01051102

THE SAMURAI WERE THUGS IN FROCKS WITH STUPID HAIRCUTS, AND HAIKU POEMS ARE LIMERICKS THAT DON'T MAKE YOU LAUGH.

PHOTOGRAPHY BY LAURA EDWARDS

JAPANEASY

TIM ANDERSON

Hardie Grant
BOOKS

ZANUSSI

INTRODUCTION

Japanese cuisine: loved and respected the world over for its emphasis on rare, top-quality ingredients, precise cooking techniques, and its adherence to strict traditions dating back centuries.

That's the image, anyway. But you want to know the truth?

Japanese food is *easy*.

What are your favourite Japanese dishes? Sushi? Surprisingly easy. Gyoza? Very easy. *Karaage*? Soooooo easy! Tempura? Stupidly easy. Yakitori, yakisoba, miso soup? Easy, easy, easy.

I totally get that Japanese food can be intimidating – it's true that it features a lot of unusual ingredients that are often difficult to source (not to mention pronounce). And it has a reputation for requiring an exacting level of technique developed over years and years of study and practice. And while this is true for advanced or high-end Japanese cookery, you may be surprised at how many of your favourite Japanese dishes can be satisfactorily reproduced at home, even by novices with limited access to Japanese ingredients. In fact, many Japanese recipes require no specialist ingredients at all!

This book is designed as an introduction to the world of Japanese cooking via some of its most accessible (but authentic) dishes. But the recipes here do not 'cheat' in any way – none of them require inadequate substitutions for obscure ingredients, and none will suffer from lack of experience. Rather, I have chosen recipes that are by their very nature easy to produce, from the sourcing of ingredients straight through prep and cooking. If you are looking to replicate your favourite 20-hour pork broth ramen with all the toppings at home, look elsewhere – that will never be easy (although it isn't really difficult, either). But if you are looking for fun, simple, relatively quick and, most importantly, *really delicious* Japanese dishes that you can actually make on a regular basis – this is your book.

GETTING STARTED

EXCUSES, EXCUSES

You love Japanese food. I know you do, because you're reading this book! And also because EVERYBODY loves Japanese food. It's delicious! You love Japanese food, and yet you never cook it at home. WHY? Here are some ~~reasons~~ excuses I frequently hear. Perhaps you have used them – but NOT ANY MORE. You can cook Japanese food, and you can cook it today!

I CAN'T GET JAPANESE INGREDIENTS!

YES YOU CAN !

First of all, quite a lot of Japanese recipes don't require anything more obscure than soy sauce. Tempura, for example, is just flour, cornflour, eggs, sparkling water, oil, and good veg or seafood. But Japanese staple ingredients are everywhere these days – even if you don't live anywhere near an East Asian supermarket, you will be able to find the majority of what you need at any ordinary, big supermarket. And if I'm wrong, and your local big supermarket doesn't even have rice vinegar? Or if you don't even *have* a local big supermarket? Then there is still one magical source for all things Japanese to which you can always turn…

THE INTERNET !!!

The internet is a fantastical wonderland of ingredients, Japanese and otherwise. Between online supermarkets, mega-market-places like Amazon or eBay, and smaller, specialist retailers, there are really too many sources of Japanese foods to name. They will deliver virtually anywhere in the country, often in a shorter time and for less money than you might expect. I live in London, where Japanese ingredients are relatively easy to find, but even so, I often find that online suppliers are simply the most convenient way to buy miso, seaweed, *sake*, or anything else I need to make a Japanese feast. Let me put it this way: you can order literally *everything* you need to make literally *everything* in this book ON YOUR PHONE while waiting for the bus!

THAT'S AMAZING! WHAT A TIME TO BE ALIVE!

I'VE HEARD ABOUT SUSHI CHEFS THAT SPEND TWO YEARS JUST LEARNING HOW TO COOK RICE. JAPANESE FOOD IS TOO DIFFICULT.

NO, IT ISN'T!

Not only is most Japanese food easy, it's also *fun*! Alright, so you're probably not going to be able to recreate the kind of Michelin-starred sushi dinner you may have seen prepared by a spry octogenarian and his two harassed sons. It is true that the highest level Japanese cookery – just like any kind of cookery – can only be produced by someone with years of experience under their belt. But don't let that put you off! Nobody, least of all yourself, should expect you to be able to cook like the Japanese masters, and besides, *you don't have to cook at that level* if all you're after is pure deliciousness. There is an enormous array of Japanese dishes that are so easy, a trained monkey could (probably) make them.

Forget about fancy knife-work, tricky techniques or complicated recipes – you don't need any of them to make some seriously tasty Japanese food.

I HARDLY HAVE TIME TO COOK ANYTHING AT ALL, AND JAPANESE FOOD TAKES AGES TO MAKE!

NO, IT DOESN'T!

Many Japanese recipes require only a handful of different ingredients to prep, and because ovens are uncommon in Japanese homes and there's not much of a stewing or braising tradition there, cooking methods tend to be fast: think boiling, grilling or frying. In fact, a rounded and satisfying Japanese meal can be produced from just one basic recipe and barely half an hour of combined prep and cooking time. For example:

STEP 1: Get some rice on the boil.
(5 minutes of prep, 20 minutes of cooking)

STEP 2: While the rice is cooking, whip up a quick Sweet Miso Sauce (page 175). Rub this into fillets of fish or chicken and grill them.
(10–20 minutes total)

STEP 3: Knock together a quick salad with soy sauce, sugar, lemon juice and a little sesame oil as a dressing.
(5 minutes)

STEP 4 (BONUS): Make miso soup!
(From a packet is fine, this ain't the Ritz.)
(2 minutes)

And BOOM – you're having a delicious Japanese meal at home! AND ON A WEEKDAY! And it's *even faster* if you make big batches of go-to sauces and seasonings (page 168) to have on hand for whenever that Japanese craving strikes.

You have no excuse!

LET'S COOK!!!

mizkan
ほんてり
澤之鶴
mizkan
Original
RICE
VINEGAR
for Recipes
& Cooking
Soy Sauce
MISO
TASTY
Organic Unpasteurised
AKA RED
MISO PASTE
Organic Unpasteurised
MISO PASTE
SATISFACTION
シマヤだしの素
かつお
だし
Best before date Method of display : YYYY.MM.DD
みそ汁/MISO SOUP

THE SEVEN JAPANESE INGREDIENTS YOU WILL NEED TO COOK (ALMOST) EVERYTHING IN THIS BOOK

One of the wonderful things about Japanese cooking is that in many cases, simplicity is inherent. So many traditional Japanese preparations are actually quite minimal: fresh produce, simply prepared, seasoned with just a few highly flavourful ingredients, and cooked quickly – or not cooked at all. A classic example of this is sashimi: top-quality seafood, sliced, served with soy sauce. That's it! How lovely.

In fact, whenever I get my hands on a really beautiful piece of fish, I can't resist slicing off a tiny bit to enjoy raw, dipped in a spot of soy sauce. It is one of life's simplest, purest gastronomic pleasures, like burrata with sea salt and olive oil, or really potent French cheese with really old French wine.

Of course, Japanese recipes aren't always as simple as sashimi, but more often than not they start with a similarly short list of ingredients. I don't know about you, but I'm pretty intimidated by cooking Thai or Indian curries at home, mainly because they often require a huuuuuge amount of herbs, spices and other seasonings. Japanese food is rarely like that. Mainly it is about a handful of fresh ingredients being introduced to a handful of amenable seasonings and just letting them mingle. And there aren't too many of those amenable seasonings that you'll need to have on hand to cook a very wide range of dishes. Start with these:

1

SOY SAUCE

Soy sauce adds **salt**, **umami** and a little **acidity** to dishes – I always compare the flavour profile to less-intense Marmite. I season nearly all my cooking, Japanese or otherwise, with a little bit of soy sauce in addition to or instead of salt, because of the rich, satisfying depth it provides. Try it in a bolognese, or in a caramel sauce!

Chances are you already have soy sauce at home. However, you should make sure you use a Japanese soy sauce rather than a Chinese one, as the flavour can be remarkably different. Kikkoman is the most widely available brand, and it is quite good. It is a little bit more expensive than some, but the quality is superior. At a pinch, Chinese light soy sauce will do in most preparations. I rarely use dark soy sauce in Japanese cooking because of its powerful, molasses-y intensity, but even that is fine in some meatier recipes.

2

MIRIN

Mirin adds **sweetness** to dishes, and is comparable to very light honey in flavour (but it's much less viscous). It is a kind of fortified, highly sweetened sake – nothing you'd ever want to drink, but it is essential to the sweet-and-salty flavour profile found in many Japanese dishes. In European cookery very few ingredients are used to add sweetness to savoury dishes, but next time you think a dish needs a little something, it may not be salt – try a splash of mirin instead. Sometimes that mellow sweetness is all it takes to round out a sauce or gravy perfectly.

RICE VINEGAR

Rice vinegar adds **acidity** to dishes, providing a lip-smacking zing and balancing out rich, fatty or sweet flavours. Japanese food isn't often outright sour; rice vinegar is generally used in small amounts as a light seasoning, as in sushi rice, where the vinegar is mainly there to get the mouth watering. As with soy sauce, try to get a Japanese rice vinegar rather than a Chinese one; Chinese rice vinegar tends to be a little more harshly acidic, whereas Japanese rice vinegar has a faint malty flavour.

DASHI

Dashi adds **umami** and, for lack of a better word, **Japaneseness** to dishes. It is essentially a light broth – actually more of an infusion, like tea – made from *kombu*, a type of dried kelp, and *katsuobushi* (page 17), which is made from smoked, fermented and dried tuna. The kombu lends dashi a briny flavour and rich, moreish umami, which is amplified by the smoky, meaty flavour of the katsuobushi. Dashi is easy to make from scratch (page 170), but katsuobushi is hard to come by, and expensive. Instead, I'd highly recommend you buy a pack of dashi powder. That may sound like a cheat, but it really does taste good (nothing like the dreaded stock cube), and if you're concerned about authenticity, not to worry; by using dashi powder you will be making dashi *exactly* how tens of millions of home cooks in Japan make it. Dashi powder is so delicious I've even seen it used in Michelin-starred kitchens. It couldn't be simpler to use – just add water, following the packet instructions.

Dashi is sometimes the front-and-centre featured component of dishes, but perhaps more often it is a foundation onto which other, more prominent flavours are built. Either way, it is *essential*. Which is annoying, because it is perhaps the one Japanese ingredient you are not likely to find at a large, mainstream supermarket. But don't worry – it is still easy to get (any East Asian grocer will have it, and it is widely available online), and this book contains many recipes that don't require it at all.

SAKE

Sake adds **umami**, **fragrance** and subtle notes of **sweetness** and **acidity** to dishes – you can think of it like Japanese white wine. Most cooking sake has a distinctly earthy aroma reminiscent of mushrooms, but its flavour is subtle and lends a rich savouriness to foods – I sometimes describe it as like a light soy sauce without the salt. Which may be difficult to wrap your head around, but what I mean is that it provides some of the same depth as soy sauce but without the big whack of tangy salinity that comes with it. For this reason it is often put to use 'diluting' sauces, to tame powerful flavours so that others may shine.

MISO

Miso is so awesome, and here's why: it adds **umami**, **sweetness**, **acidity**, **salt**, **fragrance**, **complexity**, **Japaneseness** and sometimes even **bitterness** to dishes. It is what I call a 'complete flavour' because it has so much going on and works as a wonderful seasoning all by itself. It is essentially a paste made from fermented rice and soybeans, and there are many, many, many, many, many, many, MANY kinds of miso out there. But the types you are most likely to encounter are white (*shiro*) miso and red (*aka*) miso.

White miso is not aged for very long, and it tends to be made with a high proportion of rice, which makes it fresh, salty, sweet and light. Red miso is aged for much longer and it has a higher proportion of soybeans (and sometimes has no rice at all, or includes other grains, like barley), which makes it richer and more complex. My advice would be to get some of both just to see what they're like, but most of the recipes here call for white miso – and that one is more common, anyway.

A note about purchasing: you will likely encounter miso soup mix, in either a paste or powder form. And while this stuff is great for miso soup (I am a big fan of the British brand Miso Tasty), it isn't a good substitute for miso in recipes – it is the wrong consistency and contains other ingredients, such as seaweed, spring onions and sesame seeds.

RICE

Rice isn't so much an ingredient as simply a staple. I read somewhere that Japanese food has no 'centre' – there are no main courses and no central ingredients – but rather a 'destination', and that destination is rice. Depending on your point of view, this is either a beautifully poetic or eye-rollingly pretentious way of saying that rice simply completes a Japanese meal. Some Japanese dishes stand alone – things like okonomiyaki, ramen or yakiudon are substantial enough to be a meal in their own right. But many others are smaller and lighter – things like pieces of grilled fish, salads and miso soup – and a bowlful of rice is required to round out the meal and ensure satiety.

For me, using any kind of rice other than Japanese rice with Japanese food is just plain weird. But that may also be because Japanese rice is my fave! I love the plump, toothsome grains; I love its slight stickiness; and I love its rich aroma. In fact, the smell of Japanese rice steaming is one of my favourite smells in the world. And anyway, it's easy to get – it's typically labelled 'sushi rice' at supermarkets (for no good reason; it's not just for sushi), but you're better off buying it at an Asian grocer if you can, as it is far cheaper and tends to be better quality.

TEN MORE INGREDIENTS YOU MIGHT WANT

TOFU

There are basically two kinds of tofu you need for Japanese cooking: silken and… uh, not silken? It's tricky to name the non-silken kind because everybody seems to label it differently, but perhaps most commonly as 'block' tofu. Silken tofu comes in little Tetra Paks that have to be snipped open at the seams, while block tofu is packaged submerged in water in plastic tubs. Silken tofu is extremely delicate (don't be fooled by the 'firm' silken tofu; it ain't that firm), so it's best in raw dishes like Hiyayakko (page 81) or in dishes where it's not cooked or handled with much movement (like miso soup). Block tofu is denser and more robust, so it holds up better in stir-fries or hot pots.

TOASTED SESAME SEEDS

Sesame seeds are almost always sold raw, which I find irksome. Raw sesame seeds taste like paper. But *toasted* sesame seeds are SO delicious! They're all nutty and rich and like a million times better than they are raw. So you have two options: buy them already toasted (any Chinese supermarket will sell them this way), or toast them yourself. The easiest way to do this is in a carefully watched dry frying pan (skillet) over a medium heat. Keep the seeds moving and pull them off the heat when they are golden brown and smell delicious.

NORI, WAKAME & FRIENDS

Who'd have thought seaweed could be such a versatile foodstuff? The Japanese, that's who. They harvest a huge variety of seaweeds for various purposes, but the two you're most likely to encounter are nori and wakame. Nori is sold as dried, dark green sheets, most commonly used to wrap sushi rolls, but it can also be snipped with scissors into fine shreds to add a lovely 'sea breeze' aroma to dishes. Wakame is sold dehydrated, and after a soak in cold water it becomes supple and silky and tender and, I think, healthy, but don't quote me on that. It's most commonly found in miso soup and similar brothy dishes, but also in Japanese salads. A couple of others to keep your eye out for are *hijiki* (a bit like wakame but smaller and nuttier) and *aonori* (a bit like nori but greener, more intense, and sold as flakes).

SHIITAKE, SHIMEJI & FRIENDS

Nowadays big supermarkets are actually a pretty good source for Japanese mushrooms, including *shiitake*, *shimeji*, *enoki* and *eringi*.

Shiitake are meaty and intense, and need to be de-stemmed before using. Shimeji are often sold as beech mushrooms, and resemble (and taste like) an elongated chestnut mushroom, but with a firmer texture. Enoki are the long, skinny ones that become almost noodly when cooked, while eringi (my favourite) are like oyster mushrooms on steroids – meaty, sweet and full of mushroomy juice. Most, if not all, of these mushrooms are typically found in those 'exotic' mushroom packs at the supermarket, which is a great way to try them all.

NOODLES

This is the definitive Japanese noodle power ranking:

RAMEN, THE ONE TRUE KING OF NOODLES

SOBA

UDON

WEIRD OBSCURE ONES LIKE SOMEN AND SHIRATAKI

Just kidding. They all have their charms, of course, but I do think you can tell a lot about a person by which noodle they prefer. If you like ramen, you're a charismatic go-getter and sensation-seeker who likes to party and experiment with psychotropic drugs. If you like *soba*, you're more of an introvert who prefers to stay home with your cat, drinking tea and watching pensive documentaries about typeface design. If you like *udon*, you're a lovelorn romantic perpetually in need of a hug.

But perhaps more accurately: if you like ramen, you like thin wheat noodles with a springy texture. If you like soba, you like thin buckwheat noodles with a nutty flavour and delicate bite. If you like udon, you like big, fat, chewy wheat noodles, so chunky they're almost like dumplings.

Soba is almost exclusively sold dried, and most brands are pretty good, but look for noodles that have a visible grain in them from the buckwheat. Udon is sold dried, fresh or frozen, and I'd strongly advise you to avoid dried – they just aren't fat enough, and tend to have a soft, sad texture. Ramen is characterised by its alkaline salts that affect gluten, giving them a characteristic 'bouncy' texture. Fresh is best, but if that's not an option, go for instant ramen. For some reason it has a better texture than dried ramen, and you can use the little seasoning packets to sprinkle on popcorn or oven chips (sooo goooood).

KOMBU

Kombu is dried kelp, and the essential ingredient in dashi – and therefore, the backbone of Japanese cookery. Steeping kombu in warm water releases its briny flavour and a powerful, lip-smacking, mouth-watering, tummy-filling umami (basically, it's full of natural MSG) that makes so much Japanese food so satisfying even when it's quite light. However, if you don't plan on making dashi from scratch (page 170), kombu won't be of much use to you. But it's worth getting a pack just to try – I find its meaty flavour to be a wonderful helper in the kitchen, especially in hearty comfort-food dishes like stews and soups.

7

KATSUOBUSHI

Katsuobushi is the *other* essential ingredient in dashi, and it delivers a strongly 'Japanese' flavour of concentrated fish. And that's basically what it is: loins of smallish tuna (*katsuo*) are smoked, fermented and dried until they resemble a chunk of fishy driftwood, then shaved into fine, papery flakes (*bushi*). It has a very moreish smoked fish flavour that will be familiar to you from a number of Japanese broths and sauces. It is also used as a topping for certain dishes, adding an umami boost as well as a striking appearance – it seems to dance and flutter when currents of hot, tasty food vapour rise off the dish it's adorning.

PANKO

Panko (literally 'bread particles') are Japanese dried breadcrumbs, characterised by a coarser, airier texture than Western breadcrumbs. They really are superior, so if you're making tonkatsu or croquettes, seek them out – you can even find them at some big supermarkets.

9

SESAME OIL

Just a few drops of toasted sesame oil is enough to impart a rich, meaty nuttiness to dishes – you won't often find it used in great quantities in Japanese cuisine (except in Sesame Sauce, page 183), but it really rounds out the flavours of Chinese-influenced dishes and hearty stir-fries like Stir-Fried Pork with Ginger Sauce (page 114) and Fried Rice (page 136).

10

PICKLED GINGER

There are two types of pickled ginger: red and pink (or white). The pale pink stuff is pretty much exclusively used as a palate-cleanser with sushi, whereas the red stuff (called *beni shoga*) is found in all sorts of dishes – it has a special affinity with Sweet Soy Sauce (page 173) and Tonkatsu Sauce (page 182) which makes it excellent (indispensible, actually) with Yakisoba (page 156).

HOW TO COOK JAPANESE RICE

There is a wide range of Japanese dishes that are not eaten with rice, but there's an even wider range of dishes that are. Rice in Japanese cooking is kind of like bread or potatoes in European cooking, mainly there to soak up sauces and provide bulk, but also beautiful in its own right when it's perfectly made – all warm and plump and sticky and steamy… wait, what were we talking about? Oh yeah. Rice.

Japanese rice cooks by absorption rather than by simple boiling, which requires slightly more precise measuring, but the cooking itself is still dead easy. First of all: know your measurements! I like to use scales to measure rice – I find it makes things a little bit more accurate, and also easier, because I can just measure everything out into the pan I'm using to cook it instead of dealing with cups and jugs.

If you're cooking rice as a side dish, you'll need about **75 g (2½ oz/ generous ⅓ cup) uncooked rice per portion**, or a little bit less for kids. For a main dish, you'll need more like **100 g (3½ oz/½ cup) per portion**. Weigh out **at least 150 g (5 oz/¾ cup) rice** to start with, and place it in a small saucepan with a snug-fitting lid.

Next: wash the rice! What you're doing here is removing excess starch, which can make the rice overly sticky and leave a pasty flavour. Using plenty of water, rub the rice between your fingers, rough it up a bit and swish the water around. Have fun with it – I often find this step therapeutic. Drain off the water, refill it, and repeat three times or so – you're looking for the water to clarify as more and more starch is washed away. It will never be *pristinely* clear – just get it down to a light haze rather than a thick fog.

Now you add your water – the ratio that works for me is **1.3 times the amount of rice, by weight** – so for 150 g (5 oz/¾ cup) rice, you'd add 195 g/ml (scant 7 oz/generous ¾ cup) water (this is roughly equivalent to **1.1 times the amount of rice in volume**, by the way). Swirl the pan to distribute the rice grains in an even layer at the bottom of the pan. Place the pan on a small burner on a high heat and bring it to the boil. Now reduce the heat to as low as possible and put the lid on the pan. Set a timer for 15 minutes, and now **forget about the rice** – opening the lid once won't ruin it, but if you do it too often, too much moisture will escape and you'll end up with rice that's either undercooked or burnt – or both! Not ideal. So resist the urge to check on your rice until the timer's up.

Kill the heat, take the lid off, take a moment to enjoy the nutty aroma billowing from the pan (ahhhhh) and then fluff the rice with a fork or chopsticks to aerate and redistribute the grains. Put the lid back on the pan and let it sit for about 5 minutes for the rice to soak up any remaining moisture (the condensation that occurs as the steam cools will also help dissolve rice starch that may be stuck to the bottom of the pan, so the rice releases more easily and the pan is easier to clean).

That's it! You now have a steaming hot pan of delicious and aromatic Japanese rice on which to build a multitude of Japanese meals.

HOW TO SERVE A JAPANESE MEAL

There are essentially three kinds of Japanese meals:

ONE BIG THING

ONE BIG THING WITH A FEW LITTLE THINGS AROUND IT

MANY LITTLE THINGS

How to serve dishes in category 1 is pretty straightforward: put the big thing in a bowl or on a plate and enjoy! Meals in this category include ramen, udon, soba, Japanese pasta, yakiudon, fried rice, rice bowls, okonomiyaki and curries. These dishes are substantial enough to satisfy on their own; they're the Japanese equivalent of a bowl of pasta or a stew.

Dishes in category 2 are substantial by themselves, but don't contain a carbohydrate such as rice or noodles for bulk, so they're not quite as satisfying on their own. They are frequently shared communally, especially in the case of hotpot dishes, and can easily be made into a meal with the addition of a bowl of rice, a salad and/or miso soup.

Category 3 includes salads, warm vegetable preparations, small grilled items like yakitori, and snacky, frequently deep-fried items like karaage or croquettes. You definitely need a few of them to make a meal.

But actually these categories exist in a sort of Venn diagram rather than in three distinct columns. For example, some people will have gyoza and a bowl of rice alongside their ramen or udon. Some people (like me) will be happy to eat loads and loads and LOADS of gyoza, by themselves, until they are sated. (I love gyoza.) And in some cases, a few big dishes are shared communally among a small group. How you decide to serve your Japanese meal kind of depends on how many people you're cooking for, and how much time you have. But here are some examples of full, satisfying Japanese meals that can be produced quickly and easily:

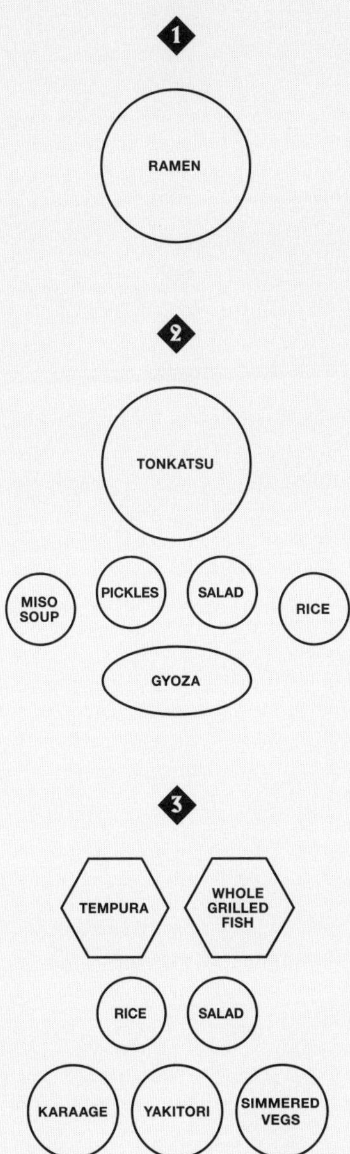

This book is divided, broadly, into small dishes and big dishes. The small dishes will require something like a rice-salad-miso soup combo to turn them into a meal, but this can be achieved in many ways – like a massive bowl of fried rice to share, with a few skewers on the side.

SWEET SOY
SWEET MISO

A FAMILY BUSINESS SINCE 1880
INGREDIENTS
JP
bière BIRRA
ALE BREWED WITH NATURAL FLAVORS

EVERYDAY SALADS

1

惣菜

You don't have to prepare a full-on feast to enjoy Japanese food at home on a regular basis. Many Japanese dishes are perfectly compatible with other kinds of home cooking, and this chapter contains several recipes that will work alongside just about any kind of meal you're having. One or two of these dishes alongside a soup, stew, a piece of grilled fish or roast meat can be your go-to recipes to add a Japanese flourish to everyday meals and satisfy your workday *washoku* (Japanese cuisine) cravings.

SIDES & SNACKS

THE BEST EDAMAME

SERVES 2

DIFFICULTY

Soy not difficult

250 g (9 oz/½ bag) frozen edamame
1 tablespoon black sesame seeds, crushed (white sesame seeds will do if you can't get black)
1 teaspoon sesame oil (optional)
a few pinches of salt, ideally sea salt

I never really understood the appeal of *edamame*. I mean, yeah, they're fine, and kinda fun to eat, but at the end of the day they're just beans, right? That's what I thought, until I changed the way I cooked them. Forget boiling – the best edamame are *grilled* (broiled). Preparing edamame with hot, dry heat dries them out slightly, making their texture more dense, and giving them a slightly caramelised, richer, nuttier aroma and flavour. They have a natural sweetness to them, making them as moreish as a tube of Pringles and way more healthy. Make a big batch and chow down while binge-watching Netflix.

METHOD

Spread the edamame out on a baking tray and place under the grill (broiler) on its highest setting. Keep checking every 5 minutes or so, turning and moving the edamame around periodically to ensure even browning. They are done when they're nicely browned (and a little bit black in some places). Immediately toss the edamame with the crushed sesame seeds, sesame oil, if using, and salt, and enjoy while piping hot.

THE BEST MISO SOUP

SERVES 2–4

Miso soup is like a bacon sandwich: even when it's bad, it's still pretty good. Instant miso soup from a packet is totally fine, but next-level from-scratch miso soup is nearly as easy to prepare, so you may as well upgrade!

METHOD

Combine the miso, dashi and mirin in a saucepan and bring to the boil. Cut the white part of the spring onions into pieces 1 cm (½ in) thick, and add those to the pan. Finely slice the green parts of the spring onions and reserve for the garnish.

Reduce the soup to a simmer, add the wakame and/or spinach and cook for just a minute or two. Now is a good time to add any embellishments you might like – for example, asparagus in the spring, courgettes in the summer, diced squash in the autumn, kale in the winter, and mussels or scallops pretty much anytime. These are strictly optional but they will add another dimension of flavour and texture to your miso soup and make it that much more satisfying. Cook for just a few more minutes until the veg or shellfish are cooked through and tender (but not soft).

Add the lemon peel and remove from the heat. Divide the tofu into deep bowls, pour over the soup and garnish with the sliced green spring onions and sesame seeds.

DIFFICULTY

Not at all difficult

4 tablespoons miso – use a red or barley miso if you can
500 ml (17 fl oz/2 cups) dashi
1 tablespoon mirin
2 spring onions (scallions)
2 tablespoons dried wakame or a handful of fresh spinach (or both)
embellishments, such as asparagus, courgettes (zucchini), squash or kale, cut into pieces slightly smaller than bite-sized, or mussels, scallops, etc. (optional)
1 cm (½ in) strip of lemon peel, white pith removed, cut into fine shreds
350 g (12 oz) block of firm silken tofu, cut into bite-sized cubes
2 pinches of toasted sesame seeds

ASAZUKE

JAPANESE QUICK PICKLES

MAKES ENOUGH FOR 2 × 500 ML (1 PINT) JARS OF TIGHTLY PACKED VEG

DIFFICULTY

Totes
not difficult

- 100 ml (3½ fl oz/scant ½ cup) water
- 10 g (½ oz) kombu or ¼ teaspoon dashi powder
- 100 g (3 ½ oz/½ cup) sugar – caster (superfine) sugar is fine but golden caster is better
- 1 teaspoon salt
- 400 ml (13 fl oz/generous 1½ cups) rice vinegar
- pinch of dried chilli flakes, or 1 small dried chilli cut in half lengthways
- vegetables: cucumbers, radishes, fennel, turnips, carrots, etc. – as much as will fit in the jars

I love pickles. I'm not a creature of routine, and my diet is rather erratic, but I actually eat some kind of pickle every single day. I eat spicy pickled bamboo shoots as a pick-me-up; pickled ginger as a garnish; and pickled fennel and cucumbers just because I can't resist them. Many Japanese pickles take days, if not weeks or months, to ferment, but the quick vinegar-brined pickles known as *asazuke* are actually among my favourites. They are sharp and salty and have a very clean, pure flavour that works well alongside all kinds of meals, not just Japanese. Also, they are superb with sake or beer – their mouth-watering acidity will keep you quaffing, so they're excellent fodder for an evening of raucous drunken board gaming. (See also: The Best Edamame, page 27.)

METHOD

Combine the water and kombu or dashi powder in a saucepan and bring to a simmer. Stir in the sugar and salt until they dissolve, then remove from the heat and combine with the rice vinegar. Add the chilli flakes or chilli.

All you have to do now is prepare your veg – pretty much any veg you like. If you want your pickles FAST, slice them into small pieces so they absorb the brine more quickly. If you can wait for your pickles, I'd recommend keeping your veg whole or just cutting them into fairly big chunks, but that's mainly so you can slice them as needed, which makes them look a bit prettier. Anyway, if you cut your veg small, the pickles will be ready in 1–2 hours. If you cut them big, they'll be ready in 4–8 hours. Either way, they'll keep in the brine for months in the fridge.

A note about radishes: if you're using them, the pink of their skins will bleed out into the brine and make ALL your pickles that colour, which some find really cool but others find off-putting.

SIMMERED GREEN VEGETABLES WITH SESAME DRESSING

SERVES 4

DIFFICULTY

Not at all difficult

200–300 g (7–10½ oz) tender green vegetables, such as green beans, asparagus, Tenderstem broccoli, runner beans or kale
about 500 ml (17 fl oz/2 cups) dashi, or water with a healthy glug each of soy sauce and mirin added
½ quantity Sesame Sauce (page 183)
pinch of toasted sesame seeds

This is one of my all-time favourite ways to prepare seasonal vegetables – an absolute classic of Japanese home cooking, and with good reason: it's ridiculously delicious.

METHOD

Trim the vegetables of any stems or tough bits. Bring the dashi or seasoned water to a high simmer and add the veg; they should cook until just tender, retaining their colour and a bit of a bite. Check them after 5 minutes and then every minute or two after that until cooked to your liking. Drain and top with the sesame sauce and sesame seeds.

MIXED SALAD WITH SWEET ONION AND GINGER DRESSING

SERVES 4

DIFFICULTY

Not at all difficult

In Japan, this dressing (or minor variations thereof) is called *wafu* dressing – literally, 'Japanese style'. It's an absolutely lovely, moreish and, most importantly, easy dressing to Japanify any kind of everyday salad you typically enjoy.

Sweet onion and ginger dressing

¼ onion
1 cm (½ in) piece of fresh ginger, peeled
100 ml (3½ fl oz/scant ½ cup) soy sauce
4 tablespoons vegetable oil
4 tablespoons rice vinegar
25 g (scant 1 oz) caster (superfine) or granulated (raw) sugar
pinch of freshly ground black pepper

Mixed salad

200 g (7 oz) mixed leaves – the dressing is sweet, so I like this with salad that has a hint of bitterness, like watercress, rocket (arugula), radicchio, endive or just good ol' lettuce
2 tomatoes, each cut into 8 wedges, or a handful of cherry tomatoes, halved
½ cucumber, sliced on the bias
handful of sliced radishes, (bell) peppers, avocados, or whatever else you like to put in your mouth/salad
pinch of toasted sesame seeds, to garnish

METHOD

Finely grate the onion and ginger, then combine with all the other dressing ingredients. Stir until the sugar dissolves. Alternatively, bung everything in a food processor and whizz it up until the onion and ginger are broken down.

Toss the leaves with some of the dressing, then arrange the tomatoes, cucumber and extra veg artfully around the leaves (remember: *artfully*). Spoon over a little more of the dressing and garnish with sesame seeds.

JAPANESE POTATO SALAD

SERVES 4

DIFFICULTY

Less difficult than that other potato salad you make

¼ cucumber
½ carrot, peeled
salt
500 g (1 lb 2 oz) potatoes – unlike most potato salads, fluffy, floury varieties like Maris Piper or King Edward work best
12 quails' eggs
6 cornichons
2 slices of ham, about 60–70 g (2–2½ oz) in total
100 g (3½ oz) mayonnaise
¼ teaspoon dashi powder
¼ teaspoon mustard
pinch of freshly ground pepper
½ bunch of chives, finely chopped

In some areas, 'Japanese' is synonymous with 'superlative'. Customer service. Trains. Lunch boxes. Therapy robots. Karaoke machines. Beauty found in the sadness of impermanence and imperfection.

And I would add potato salad to that list – Japanese potato salad is just the best. For the uninitiated, it is distinguished by three key components: salty-umami additions such as ham and MSG; thinly sliced crunchy vegetables; and potatoes that are roughed up, almost mashed, to create a light and creamy texture.

By the way, if you can get Kewpie mayo, a Japanese brand that is exceedingly delicious, feel free to use that instead of the mayo recipe provided below.

METHOD

Slice the cucumber and carrot in half lengthways, then slice both very, very thinly – use a mandoline if you have one (watch your fingers!). Sprinkle these with salt and let them sit for about 20 minutes to tenderise, then rinse them under cold running water to remove the salt.

Meanwhile, peel the potatoes and cut into chunks, about 3 cm (generous 1 in) thick, similar to how you would prepare them for roasting. Transfer to a saucepan, cover with about 2.5 cm (1 in) water and add a big pinch of salt, then bring to a high simmer and cook until tender to the point of a knife. Remove the taters with a slotted spoon (keep the water) and leave to dry out and cool completely.

Bring the water to a rolling boil and add the quails' eggs. Cook for 3 minutes and drain, then transfer to cold water to stop the cooking. Peel the eggs and cut them in half. Dice the cornichons and cut the ham into thin strips.

Combine the mayonnaise, dashi powder, mustard, pepper and a pinch of salt. Using a fork or sturdy whisk, mix this into the cooked and cooled potatoes with unnecessary roughness – you want to break up the potatoes and sort of half-mash them to give the salad a fluffy, creamy texture. Mix in the cucumber, carrots, cornichons, ham and quails' eggs. Taste and adjust the seasoning to your liking, then serve, topped with chopped chives. Perfect with tonkatsu (page 120) or karaage (page 61).

CABBAGE WITH SWEET GINGER VINEGAR

SERVES 4

DIFFICULTY

Absurdly
not difficult

At restaurants and bars in Japan, it's not uncommon to be handed a little dish of complimentary something or other when you sit down, as a sign of hospitality and to whet your appetite before ordering. My favourite of these little freebies is cabbage with a sweet vinegar dressing. 'That's boring,' you're probably thinking. 'NEXT RECIPE, PLEASE.' But wait! What if I told you that Japanese cabbage is really sweet and delicious? And that the dressing it's dressed with is even MORE sweet and delicious? PLEASE KEEP READING. I PROMISE: THIS RECIPE IS MORE EXCITING THAN IT SOUNDS. Okay, so here's the deal: cabbage is not sexy, but if you choose good cabbage and serve it with this dressing, then it comes pretty close.

80 ml (2¾ fl oz/⅓ cup) vinegar
3 tablespoons mirin
10 g (½ oz) caster (superfine) sugar
30 g (1 oz) fresh ginger, finely sliced (don't bother peeling it)
2 tablespoons soy sauce
2 tablespoons dashi
1 teaspoon Tonkatsu Sauce (page 182), ketchup or brown sauce
½ sweet cabbage (hispi/sweetheart/pointed/flat)
pinch of toasted sesame seeds, to garnish

METHOD

Combine the vinegar, mirin, sugar, ginger, soy sauce and dashi in a saucepan and bring to a simmer. Remove from the heat and leave to infuse for about 20 minutes, then remove and discard the ginger. Stir in the tonkatsu sauce, ketchup or brown sauce. Chop the cabbage into roughly bite-sized pieces, dress with the ginger vinegar and garnish with sesame seeds.

DAIGAKU IMO

CANDIED SWEET POTATO WEDGES

SERVES 4

This dish is called *daigaku imo* in Japanese, which means 'university potato'. It got that name because of its popularity among broke college students who don't really know how to cook. The ingredients are cheap, the cooking is easy, and its sweet-savoury flavour makes for a highly satisfying snack. But what's really great about it is its versatility: it's nice on its own, but it also makes a great side dish and even a dessert. Use purple sweet potatoes if you can get them, as the texture is a little bit firmer, but if not, the orange kind will still be delicious.

DIFFICULTY

This dish was invented for college students, by college students, which is to say: not at all difficult

oil, for shallow-frying
2 big sweet potatoes (300–350 g/ 10½–12 oz each), washed and cut into bite-sized wedges
4 tablespoons sugar, ideally golden caster (superfine) or light brown
2 tablespoons golden syrup
1 tablespoon soy sauce
grated zest and juice of 1 lime
1 tablespoon black sesame seeds, crushed
pinch of sea salt

METHOD

Pour enough oil into a deep, wide frying pan (skillet) to cover the base with a thin layer, and set over a medium heat. When the oil is hot, add the sweet potatoes and cook until golden brown and soft in the centre, stirring frequently, about 8 minutes.

Meanwhile, gently melt together the sugar, golden syrup, soy sauce and lime juice in a separate saucepan large enough to hold all your potato wedges. When the potatoes are done and the sugar syrup is melted and bubbly, transfer the potatoes into the syrup with a slotted spoon and stir to combine.

Remove from the heat and spread the potatoes out on a lightly oiled or buttered tray. Sprinkle with the sesame seeds, sea salt and lime zest. Leave to cool slightly before serving.

TOMATO SALAD WITH SPICY PONZU

SERVES 4

DIFFICULTY

Embarrassingly not difficult

Show of hands: who knows what umami is?

(Many hands up.)

Okay, now show of hands: who *really* knows what umami is?

(Nervous smiles, shifty eyes, many hands slowly lowered.)

Let me explain! Umami is a basic taste. You've all heard of salty, bitter, sweet and sour – the four basic tastes we all learnt about as kids – but now we know there is at least one more, and that's umami. Umami is *savouriness*, and its status as a basic taste was confirmed by the Japanese chemical scientist Kikunae Ikeda in 1908 – it's got a Japanese name solely because it was discovered by a Japanese man, not because it is specifically Japanese in any way. So why are we just learning about it now, a full century later? Well, partly because compared to the other basic tastes, umami is quite subtle and difficult to pinpoint. The others are quite obvious and upfront – umami is more of a backdrop, a bass line rather than a melody. But it is absolutely essential to delicious food, which is why cultures the world over celebrate ingredients that are umami-amplifiers. These include dashi and soy sauce in Japan, cheese and bacon in Britain, and tomatoes and red wine in Italy (to name a few).

Umami is NOT a Japanese thing, nor is it some kind of mystical über-taste caused by a perfect balance of all other tastes, as I so often hear. Umami is universal, and it's easy to incorporate into your food – especially because umami compounds work synergistically and build on each other, which can make food taste extremely deep and moreish.

One very easy way to experience this is in the simple combination of tomatoes and soy sauce. Both are naturally very umami, but together they're like an umami love-in, bringing out each other's rich sweetness. This recipe builds on that with a little citrus to accent the tomatoes' tang and a little kick of chilli as well. Very simple, but oh so delicious.

200 ml (7 fl oz/scant 1 cup) Ponzu (page 176)
1 teaspoon Tabasco or sriracha or similarly hot chilli sauce (or more or less, to taste)
10 g (½ oz) caster (superfine) or granulated (raw) sugar
2 teaspoons sesame oil
500–600 g (1 lb 2 oz–1 lb 5 oz) tomatoes, cut into halves or quarters – try to get a variety of sizes and colours if you can
bunch of chives, finely chopped
½ teaspoon toasted sesame seeds
10–12 fresh basil leaves, torn (optional)

METHOD

Stir together the ponzu, hot sauce, sugar and sesame oil until the sugar dissolves. Toss the tomatoes in this mixture – you can eat them fresh right then, but they're even better after soaking in the dressing for a while (an hour will do, but overnight is even better). To serve, simply dish out the tomatoes and top with the chives, sesame seeds and basil, if using.

ZAKKOKU-MAI

MULTIGRAIN RICE

MAKES ABOUT 1 KG (2 LB 3 OZ) UNCOOKED RICE

DIFFICULTY

Not very difficult

Whenever I go back to Japan, it's lovely to be reminded of all the minutiae and miscellany of day-to-day life there, the little details that made my whole experience as an expat so rich and absorbing. Things like the pleasant melodies that play before train doors close, the weird hangover remedy drinks they sell at convenience stores, and mundane supermarket staples – not the exciting stuff like fresh yuzu or sashimi-grade yellowtail, but the ordinary, taken-for-granted stuff like *zakkoku* rice.

Zakkoku means multigrain, and zakkoku rice is Japanese white rice mixed with a handful of various seeds, grains and pulses. I didn't actually eat that much of it when I lived in Japan, seeing as I *really* like plain white rice and was surrounded by it, but I loved zakkoku rice whenever I did have it. Nowadays, I'm much more into weird grains like bulgar, millet and (God help me) quinoa. So I make big batches of zakkoku rice at home to have on hand whenever the rice craving strikes. If you have trouble finding some of these grains (you shouldn't), feel free to leave them out.

500 g (1 lb 2 oz/generous 2½ cups) Japanese rice
100 g (3½ oz/½ cup) freekeh
100 g (3½ oz/½ cup) quinoa (I like the red kind, but just for colour)
100 g (3½ oz/½ cup) buckwheat
100 g (3½ oz/½ cup) bulgar
50 g (2 oz/½ cup) rolled oats
25 g (1 oz) linseeds
25 g (1 oz) toasted sesame seeds

METHOD

Combine all the ingredients in a container with a lid and shake to combine. To cook, weigh out 75 g (2½ oz) zakkoku rice per portion (but don't do less than 150 g (5 oz) at a time, or it won't cook evenly) and put it in a small saucepan with a snug-fitting lid. Add water in a 1.5:1 ratio to the mass of the rice; if you're cooking 150 g (5 oz) rice, for example, you'll need 225 ml (8 fl oz) water. Bring the water to a low boil, then place the lid on the pan and reduce the heat to the lowest setting possible. Leave to steam, covered, for 18 minutes. Remove from the heat, fluff the rice with a fork or chopsticks, put the lid back on and leave to rest for 5 minutes before serving.

PAN-ROASTED MUSHROOMS WITH SOY-GARLIC BUTTER

SERVES 4

DIFFICULTY

I could go on and on about how not difficult this recipe is, but I don't have mushroom

- 400–500 g (14–18 oz) mushrooms – any kind will do, really, but in this recipe I like oyster best
- 1 tablespoon vegetable oil
- 100 g (3½ oz/scant 1 stick) butter
- 12 garlic cloves, peeled, bashed and roughly chopped
- 3 tablespoons soy sauce
- pinch of freshly ground black pepper
- a few drops of truffle oil (optional)

Mushrooms. Soy sauce. Garlic. Butter. Not much else to say really, other than that if those four things don't ring your bells, then I'm not sure we can be friends.

METHOD

Prepare your mushrooms into bite-sized pieces – for oyster, I just tear them up a bit; for button or chestnut, I cut them in half; for Portobello, I'd cut them into eighths.

Heat the oil in a wide frying pan (skillet) over a medium-high heat and add the mushrooms. Try to cook them in a single layer so they all brown nicely, if you can (you may want to do this in batches). When the mushrooms have taken on a lovely colour and tenderised, remove them from the pan, lower the heat and add the butter and garlic. Cook the garlic gently – very gently – until it softens and caramelises. Add the soy sauce, then add the mushrooms back to the pan and stir everything together to warm through. Finish with the black pepper and truffle oil, if using.

SIMMERED TURNIPS WITH SWEET MISO SAUCE

SERVES 2–4

I like turnips. For something so ordinary, they're surprisingly weird, with a flavour like the bastard child of a radish and a cabbage. They can be bland when cooked, but this recipe corrects for that with careful simmering in dashi and a sweet, bold miso sauce.

DIFFICULTY

Very
not difficult

4 big or 8 small turnips
400–500 ml (13–17 fl oz/ 1½–2 cups) dashi
big pinch of salt
100 ml (3½ fl oz/scant ½ cup) Sweet Miso Sauce (page 175)

METHOD

If your turnips have their greens attached, cut them off, leaving 1–2 cm (½–¾ in) attached to the root. Wash the greens and peel the roots. Cut the turnips into halves if they're small, or quarters if they're big.

Bring the dashi to a high simmer and add the salt. Blanch the turnip greens, if using, then remove with a slotted spoon and rinse them under cold running water to stop the cooking. Add the turnips to the dashi and simmer until they are just tender, with some bite left in their centres – check them after 5 minutes, and every 2–3 minutes after that. Drain well (save the dashi for future use if you like) and top with the sweet miso sauce to serve.

NASU DENGAKU

SWEET MISO-GLAZED AUBERGINE

SERVES 4

So many people I speak to name this absolute classic as one of their favourite Japanese dishes, which makes me very happy. It's not sexy like sushi, it's not complicated like ramen, and in fact it is even a little *ugly*. So I love that people get so excited about it – it's got none of the pretence or the showiness that Japanese food is often expected to have. It's just pure, concentrated deliciousness: fudgy aubergine (eggplant) with a profoundly delicious caramelised miso sauce.

METHOD

Cut the aubergines in half lengthways and score the flesh in a diamond pattern, about 5 mm (¼ in) deep (this will help them cook evenly and absorb the glaze).

Pour the oil into a deep frying pan (skillet) to a depth of about 1 cm (½ in) and heat over a medium heat. Add the aubergines and fry for about 5 minutes on each side, until the flesh has browned and softened and the skin has become glossy and brittle. Carefully remove from the oil and drain well on kitchen paper.

Spoon the sweet miso sauce onto the scored side of each aubergine and place under a hot grill for 5–10 minutes; the glaze should bubble and brown and fuse with the aubergine. Garnish with sesame seeds and serve.

DIFFICULTY

So not difficult you'll wonder why you've never made it before

2 aubergines (eggplants)
oil, for shallow-frying
120–150 ml (4–5 fl oz/½–⅔ cup) Sweet Miso Sauce (page 175)
toasted sesame seeds, to garnish

SMALL DISHES

2
一品料理

These recipes are for smallish things that won't form a full meal on their own, but can be combined with each other, or bigger dishes, or the everyday dishes from the previous chapter, to make a full meal. Basically, one of these + salad/veg + rice + miso soup (or similar combination) = delicious Japanese dinner.

GYOZA

MAKES ABOUT 40 GYOZA

Distant cousins of ravioli. Long-lost half-brothers of pasties. Grand-nephews twice removed of empanadas. Yes, the Japanese gyoza are part of a noble global family of juicy meat encapsulated in a round of folded-over dough. But they are most closely related to (and in fact, largely indistinguishable from) Chinese *jiaozi* dumplings, specifically *guotie*: potstickers. The main difference between gyoza and their Chinese ancestor is the thickness of the dough; gyoza wrappers are rolled out to a fine, pasta-like thinness, whereas jiaozi pastry is a bit more substantial. Either way, they are delicious.

Gyoza are fun and easy to make at home, and particularly easy if you can get the wrappers pre-made – they are sold frozen in East Asian supermarkets. Then it's a simple matter of bashing together the filling, assembling and frying. If you can't get the wrappers, it's still not hard, but it will take a little bit more time and effort. Making gyoza is a pleasantly meditative, repetitive task if you make them on your own, but I prefer to make them with a partner. It makes it go faster, and turns it into a fun and sociable experience. At big get-togethers in Japan, it's common to see a group of old ladies sitting around a table, making gyoza and trading gossip.

DIFFICULTY

Not difficult but it might take a little practice – don't be discouraged!!!

oil, as needed for frying
soy sauce, vinegar and chilli oil, to serve

For the wrappers

280 g (10 oz/generous 2 cups) plain (all-purpose) flour
½ teaspoon salt
120 ml (4 fl oz/½ cup) just-boiled water
cornflour (cornstarch), for dusting

For the filling

500 g (1 lb 2 oz) minced (ground) pork – not the lean stuff
½ leek, trimmed and finely diced
2 cm (¾ in) piece of fresh ginger, peeled and very finely chopped
6–10 garlic cloves (depending on your preference), very finely chopped
¾ teaspoon salt
½ teaspoon ground pepper (black is good; white is better)

METHOD

For the wrappers, sift the flour and salt together into a mixing bowl. Add the boiled water to the flour little by little, incorporating it with a spoon or spatula as you go. When all the water has been added, start working it with your hands; when it all comes together, it should be soft but not at all sticky. Sprinkle some cornflour on the work surface and tip the dough out onto it. Knead for about 10 minutes, until the dough is smooth. If you have a stand mixer with a dough hook, by all means use it, but do use your hands to make sure the dough is nice and soft and dry.

Roll the dough out into two chubby logs, about 3 cm (1¼ in) in diameter. Wrap each log in cling film (plastic wrap) and leave to rest in the fridge for 30–60 minutes. Unwrap the dough and sprinkle a little more cornflour on your work surface, then cut each log into pieces about 1 cm (½ in) across – you should get about 20 pieces out of each log.

Use your hands to roll each piece of dough into a little ball, then use a rolling pin dusted with cornflour to roll each ball out into a flat disc. Try to make them very thin, but not so thin that they become difficult to work with – 1 mm (1⁄32 in) thick is a good goal, but 2 mm (1⁄16 in) will be fine. In fact, 3 mm (1⁄10 in) will probably be fine. Just make them as thin as you are comfortable with!

Dust each wrapper with cornflour and stack them up as you go, covering the stack with a clean, damp tea towel to keep them from drying out. Oh, and don't worry if they're not perfect circles – you can still manipulate them into a nice shape when you fill and fold them. If you're not using them immediately, you can keep them wrapped in cling film in the fridge for about 3 days.

For the filling, mix the minced pork, leek, ginger, garlic, salt and pepper with your hands until everything is well incorporated. That's it.

TO ASSEMBLE AND COOK:

First of all, you will need the following things set up: a small spoon; a bowl of water, 1 or 2 baking trays lined with baking parchment and dusted with cornflour; and a non-stick frying pan (skillet) with a lid.

Let's make gyoza!

1 Lay out about 6 gyoza wrappers at a time on your worktop.
2 Use your small spoon to portion out a little bit of the filling into the centre of each wrapper.
3 Dip a finger in the water, and wet the outside edge of each wrapper.
4 Cup the wrapper in your (clean, dry) hand and fold the wrapper over the filling, pressing in the middle to seal.
5 Press down along one side of the gyoza to seal and to force the air out.
6 Press down along the other side of the gyoza to complete the seal.
7 Fold the sealed side over itself 3–5 times to form an attractive parcel (NOTE: gyoza need not be attractive to be delicious).
8 Lay the gyoza in rows on your lined trays.
9 Repeat until all the filling or wrappers are gone. (You are a gyoza master if you ration both perfectly – but if you have extra filling, just make yourself a meatball or two. Go on, you've earned it!)

Now the fun part: cooking. Gyoza cook in two ways simultaneously: frying and steaming. The trick is to get a nice, crispy bottom and a supple, tender top.

Heat a little bit of oil (1 tablespoon or so) in your non-stick pan over a medium heat. Add the gyoza in rows or a circular pattern and fry until the bottoms are golden brown – it should take about 3–5 minutes. Without turning the gyoza, add about 50 ml (2 fl oz) water to the pan and put the lid on. Let them steam for 5 minutes or so, until they're cooked through and most of the water has evaporated.

(How to tell if they're cooked through: give them a little prod on their tops. If they feel firm, they're cooked. And if you've made really beautifully thin wrappers, then you may be able to actually see through them; the meat will go from pink to pale grey when it's cooked.)

Let the remaining water evaporate from the pan to ensure crisp bottoms. When they're done, carefully lift them from the pan with a spatula, or turn them out directly onto a big, flat plate. Serve with a little bit of soy sauce, vinegar and perhaps (definitely) chilli oil for dippin'.

Oh, and by the way: in Japan it is against the law to enjoy gyoza without beer. That's how well they go together.

CHICKEN KARAAGE

JAPANESE FRIED CHICKEN

SERVES 4

DIFFICULTY

Considering this may be the best fried chicken in the world, it is incredibly not difficult

It seems fried chicken is everywhere you turn in Japan. KFCs are numerous, and the homegrown version, *karaage*, can be bought from convenience stores, ramen shops, vending machines, department store food halls, school cafeterias, supermarkets, street stalls, *izakaya* (boozers with food), train station kiosks… basically anywhere food is sold. It is *enormously* popular – and why shouldn't it be? It's just so damn delicious – all crunchy crust and hot chicken juice. It's simply exquisite – and exquisitely simple.

4 chicken thighs, boneless and skin on
cornflour (cornstarch), for dredging (if not using seasoned flour, below)
oil, for deep-frying

For the marinade
100 ml (3½ fl oz/scant ½ cup) sake
3 tablespoons mirin
3 tablespoons vinegar
3 tablespoons lime juice
2 tablespoons sriracha or similar hot chilli sauce
2 tablespoons soy sauce
1 tablespoon sesame oil
10 garlic cloves, peeled
4 shallots or 2 banana shallots, roughly chopped
15 g (½ oz) peeled fresh ginger, thinly sliced
½ teaspoon salt
¼ teaspoon pepper

For the seasoned flour (optional)
250 g (9 oz/2½ cups) cornflour (cornstarch)
1 teaspoon freshly ground pepper
1 teaspoon salt
1 teaspoon toasted sesame seeds
½ teaspoon dashi powder
¼ teaspoon chilli powder
¼ teaspoon ground ginger

METHOD

For the marinade, whizz all the ingredients together in a food processor until no big chunks remain (it doesn't have to be perfectly smooth).

Cut the chicken thighs into pieces no bigger than about 3 cm (1¼ in) at their thickest point – most thighs will yield 4 pieces, but you should get 5 or 6 out of bigger ones. The main thing to bear in mind is that they need to cook quickly, before the crust begins to burn. Basically, you should err on the side of small. Place the chicken pieces in the marinade and coat them, then leave in the fridge for at least an hour and up to 48 hours.

For the seasoned flour, if using, simply combine all the ingredients until the seasonings are well distributed.

To cook, pour at least 1 litre (34 fl oz/4 cups) oil into a very deep, wide saucepan, making sure it comes no higher than halfway up the sides, and heat to no higher than 170°C (340°F). Remove the chicken from the marinade, letting any excess drip off, and dredge in the cornflour or seasoned flour, ensuring that all the nooks and crannies are well coated – this will help maximise crust and minimise burning. Carefully drop the chicken into the oil in small batches, checking the temperature periodically to ensure it is between 160 and 170°C (320 and 340°F), and fry for 6–8 minutes. If you have a meat thermometer, use it: the chicken is done when it reaches an internal temperature of 65°C (149°F). Or use a knife to cut into the biggest piece of chicken at its thickest point. If it's pink, back into the oil it goes. If it's not pink, it's karaage time!

Drain on kitchen paper and, if you're not using the seasoned flour, finish with a little salt and pepper. This chicken is so juicy it doesn't really need a dip, but it's good with mayo, ponzu (page 176), or just good ol' soy sauce and a wedge of lime.

IKA-YAKI

GRIDDLED SQUID

SERVES 4

Whenever there's good, meaty squid at the market, it's hard for me to resist not putting this on special at the restaurant. It's so simple but so delicious, with soy sauce and the char of the griddle (or frying pan) enhancing the natural umami of fresh squid. Excellent sake fodder, too.

DIFFICULTY

Super
not difficult

4 medium squid, about 12–16 cm (4¾–6 in) long, excluding tentacles
100 ml (3½ fl oz/scant ½ cup) soy sauce
100 ml (3½ fl oz/scant ½ cup) sake
25g (1 oz) caster (superfine) sugar
1 tablespoon oil
4 teaspoons chilli oil (or more or less, to taste)
½ lemon, cut into wedges

METHOD

Clean or have your fishmonger clean the squid: cut the heads off, reserving the tentacles, gut them, remove the quills and remove any tough outer skin.

Stir together the soy sauce, sake and sugar until the sugar dissolves.

I find cooking these works best if you use 2 frying pans (skillets). Rub a little oil onto the underside of one of them with kitchen paper, and set both over a high heat. Add a little oil to the other pan, and when it's very, very hot, carefully lay the squid tubes and tentacles into the pan. At this point, lay the other hot frying pan directly on top of the squid to weigh it down and cook it from both sides. Cook this way for just 3–4 minutes, then remove the top frying pan and add the sauce.

Cook for another 2–3 minutes, until the liquid has reduced to a thin glaze and the squid is cooked through. Toss the squid through the liquid before removing to a chopping board. To serve, slice the squid into rings and pour over whatever liquid is left in the pan. Garnish with chilli oil and wedges of lemon.

EBI-FURAI

FRIED PRAWNS WITH SHICHIMI MAYO

SERVES 4

Many restaurants in the UK erroneously sell this dish as 'prawn katsu', which is wrong and stupid because *katsu* means 'cutlet'. In Japan 'prawn katsu' is a kind of prawn (shrimp) patty, breaded and deep-fried like a schnitzel – the prawns themselves, given the same treatment, are simply called *ebi furai*: fried prawns. But I guess that doesn't sound Japanese enough, or something. Anyway, it doesn't really matter how Japanese they are, or what they're called. They're just delicious, simple as that.

METHOD

To keep the prawns from curling up as they cook, slice across their underside in a series of shallow cuts. Season them with a little salt, then dredge in flour, then the beaten eggs, and finally the panko.

These can be shallow-fried or deep-fried. If shallow-frying, heat about 3 mm (1/10 in) oil in a frying pan (skillet) over a medium-high heat, and cook the prawns for about 2–3 minutes on each side.

If you're deep-frying, pour enough oil into a very deep, wide saucepan (or pot) to come no higher than halfway up the sides. Heat the oil to 190°C (375°F) and cook the prawns for 4–5 minutes. Drain on kitchen paper.

Stir the *shichimi togarashi* into the mayonnaise. To serve, prop the prawns up against the lettuce, and dollop the mayo on the side.

DIFFICULTY

Ridiculously not difficult

16–20 tiger prawns (shrimp), shelled and deveined (leave the tails on, and heads, if you like)
salt
plain (all-purpose) flour, as needed
2 eggs, beaten
200 g (7 oz/4¾ cups) panko breadcrumbs
oil, for frying
2 teaspoons Shichimi Togarashi (page 180)
150 g (5 oz) mayonnaise
1 little gem lettuce, cut into quarters

KANI KURIMU KOROKKE

CRAB CREAM CROQUETTES

MAKES 16–20 CROQUETTES

These little nuggets of seafoody goodness aren't especially Japanese in terms of flavour or technique, and yet they're among the more common izakaya (boozers with food) menu items. Which makes sense, really – they're good for sharing, good with sake, and just plain good.

You can use any kind of crab meat for this – including the fake stuff – but my recommendation for both value and flavour is a 50–50 mix of white and dark crab meat. Supermarkets and fishmongers often sell this pre-mixed in little tubs. The dark crab meat gives a lovely, strong crab flavour.

DIFFICULTY

Can be fiddly,
but not difficult

60 g (2 oz/½ stick) butter
1 onion, finely diced
6 tablespoons plain (all-purpose) flour, plus extra for dredging
450 ml (16 fl oz/1¾ cups) full-fat (whole) milk
3 tablespoons crème fraîche or sour cream
200 g (7 oz) crab meat (all white, all fake, or a mix of white, fake, and/or dark)
pinch of salt
pinch of freshly ground pepper
small pinch of chilli powder
2 eggs, beaten
250 g (9 oz/scant 6 cups) panko breadcrumbs
oil, for deep-frying – about 1 litre (34 fl oz/4 cups)
½ bunch of chives, finely chopped, to garnish
Ponzu or Tonkatsu Sauce (pages 176 and 182), to serve

METHOD

Melt the butter in a saucepan and add the onion. Fry until soft, then whisk in the flour and cook on a low-medium heat, stirring frequently, until the roux becomes amber and aromatic. Add the milk in a slow, steady stream, whisking constantly, then add the crème fraîche or sour cream and bring to a low boil. Stir in the crab meat, salt, pepper and chilli powder, then taste and adjust the seasoning to your liking.

Keep cooking the white sauce for 5 minutes or so, stirring frequently, until very thick. Pour out into a container, transfer to the fridge and leave to cool completely.

When the crabby béchamel is totally cold, it will solidify into a kind of thick paste. Rub a little oil into your hands, grab little blobs of the paste and shape into croquettes about 5 cm (2 in) long and 2½ cm (1 in) across (Japanese croquettes are bigger and more oblong than typical Spanish *croquetas*).

Roll the croquettes in flour, 3 or 4 at a time, until completely coated. Dunk them in the beaten egg, then roll them in the panko to coat completely (tip: use a slotted spoon or fork to transfer them from the egg to the panko to keep your fingers from going gummy).

Place your croquettes on a tray and put back into the fridge for 15–20 minutes to firm up again before frying. If you're not cooking these immediately, freeze them in a single layer on a tray – once hard, transfer them to a container and they will last in the freezer for several months.

Pour your oil into a very deep, wide saucepan or pot, to come no higher than halfway up the sides and, if cooking from the fridge, heat the oil to 180°C (350°F). If cooking from frozen, heat the oil to 160°C (320°F). Carefully drop the croquettes into the hot oil and fry for 6–7 minutes (longer from frozen) until the crust is golden brown. You may have to turn them over once during cooking to ensure even colour. Retrieve the croquettes with a slotted spoon and drain on kitchen paper. Garnish with chives and serve with ponzu or tonkatsu sauce.

SATSUMA-IMO KUROGOMA KOROKKE

SWEET POTATO AND SESAME CROQUETTES

MAKES 12–16 CROQUETTES

DIFFICULTY

Not difficult.
Says a-who?
Sesame

700 g (1 lb 8½ oz) sweet potatoes, peeled, diced and briefly soaked in cold water
salt
2 tablespoons each of black and white sesame seeds, toasted and crushed
200 g (7 oz/4¾ cups) panko breadcrumbs
plain (all-purpose) flour, as needed
2 eggs, beaten
oil, for deep frying, about 1 litre (34 fl oz/4 cups)
Ponzu or Tonkatsu Sauce (pages 176 and 182), to serve

Japanese croquettes, or *korokke*, are often potato-based rather than béchamel-based. This pleases me for two reasons: 1) potatoes are easier to work with than béchamel, and 2) potatoes have a nicer flavour than béchamel. And that's especially true in the case of sweet potatoes. These work well as a main on their own, or as a side dish… and, come to think of it, even as a dessert if you serve them with ice cream and maple syrup.

METHOD

Simmer the sweet potatoes in water until just tender, then drain and leave to cool and dry. Mash together with salt to taste, and half the crushed sesame seeds. If the mixture is still warm, transfer to the fridge until chilled.

Combine the remaining sesame seeds with the panko. Roll the cooled mash into croquette shapes, about 5 cm (2 in) long and 2½ cm (1 in) across, and roll these in flour, 3 or 4 at a time, until completely coated. Dunk them in the beaten egg, then roll them in the panko-sesame mixture to coat completely.

Pour your oil into a very deep, wide saucepan (or pot) to come no higher than halfway up the sides. Heat to 180°C (350°F) and fry the croquettes for about 5 minutes, until golden brown, then drain on kitchen paper. Serve with tonkatsu sauce or ponzu.

CHICKEN THIGH AND SPRING ONION YAKITORI

MAKES 8 SKEWERS

DIFFICULTY

Not difficult
at all

- 4 chicken thighs, boneless and skin on
- 8 spring onions (scallions)
- about 100–120 ml (3½–4 fl oz/ scant ½ cup) Sweet Soy Sauce (page 173)
- pinch of toasted sesame seeds, to garnish

Yakitori was always one of my favourite foods in Japan, so easy to love and easy to make that I never understood why it never caught on in the UK restaurant scene. But no matter – it's very easy to replicate at home. In Japan, the best yakitori shops take an anatomical approach to cooking chicken on sticks, butchering birds down to each constituent muscle and organ, and grilling them with precise temperatures and timings to get the most out of the bird. And that's great, if you have the time and the inclination to study galline myology. If you don't, then all you really need to know is juicy chicken + delicious sauce + hot grill = GOOD.

METHOD

Cut the chicken thighs in half lengthways, then cut each half into 4 pieces. Cut the spring onions into chunks the same width as the chicken pieces, and thread the chicken and the spring onions onto skewers, alternating spring onion, chicken, spring onion, chicken, etc. Wrap the ends of each skewer in foil.

Ideally you will cook these over charcoal or wood. But let's be real: you won't. At least not most of the time. But that's cool – they'll be nearly as delicious under the grill (broiler). Put the grill on high and position your oven rack 10–12 cm (4–5 in) or so away from the heat.

Using a pastry brush or spoon, lightly coat the skewers with the sweet soy sauce, then park them under the grill. Yakitori likes to be fussed over – it's very hands-on. Check the skewers often, turning them, re-glazing with the sauce, and moving them around, to ensure they are all cooked through and beautifully caramelised. This should take anywhere from 10 to 15 minutes total, depending on the size of the thighs and the power of your grill. When the skewers are done, give them one last brush of the sauce and garnish with sesame seeds. Enjoy with beer.

TSUKUNE

CHICKEN PATTY YAKITORI

MAKES 8 PATTIES

DIFFICULTY

Totes
not diffy

Tsukune are sometimes translated as chicken patties, sometimes as chicken meatballs, and the truth is they can be both – though I prefer them as the former. They seem to stay juicier, for some reason, but maybe that's in my head. Oh, and also they're easier, because… fewer shapes to shape.

4 skinless, boneless chicken thighs, trimmed of cartilage
2 cm (¾ in) piece of fresh ginger, peeled and finely chopped
4 garlic cloves, finely chopped
2 spring onions (scallions), finely chopped, plus 1 extra, finely sliced, to garnish
4 shiitake mushrooms, finely chopped (optional)
big pinch of freshly ground pepper
big pinch of salt
about 100–120 ml (3½–4 fl oz/ scant ¾–½ cup) Sweet Soy Sauce (page 173)

METHOD

Cut the chicken thighs into small chunks, then mince them – you can do this by hand or with a food processor. Either way, make sure they're not *too* processed – the mince should hold together when you shape it, but it shouldn't be a paste. Little chunks of meat are what we're after.

Put the grill on high and position your oven rack 10–12 cm (4–5 in) or so away from the heat.

Combine the chicken mince with the ginger, garlic, chopped spring onions, mushrooms, pepper and salt, then form into oblong patties and thread them onto skewers. Wrap the ends of the skewers in foil, apply the sweet soy sauce with a spoon or pastry brush. Grill (broil) on high for about 12–15 minutes, turning the skewers and re-applying the glaze frequently. Garnish with the sliced spring onion.

BACON-WRAPPED ASPARAGUS SKEWERS

MAKES ABOUT 8 SKEWERS

Asparagus season doesn't last very long, so you have to take advantage of it when it comes around. For me, there's hardly a better way to do so than this very simple, classic yakitori shop recipe. And when I say very simple, I *mean* very simple. In fact, I kind of feel a bit silly even including it as a recipe. But it is so good that I have to include it, even if it's just to plant the idea in your head.

DIFFICULTY

Even if this was really difficult (which it isn't), you should make them anyway because they're so good

big bunch (400–500 g/14–18 oz) of asparagus
about 15 rashers of smoked streaky bacon (dry-cured, if possible)

METHOD

If the asparagus is woody at the bottom, cut or break the ends off. Cut each stalk into batons about 3 cm (1¼ in) long. Cut each rasher of bacon into 6 small pieces. Wrap a piece of bacon around each chunk of asparagus, and thread onto skewers to secure – pack the asparagus on tightly to help hold the bacon together.

Wrap the ends of the skewers in foil and grill under a high grill, on the highest oven rack, for about 8 minutes, turning frequently. The skewers are good to go when the bacon is browned all over and the asparagus is lightly charred.

PORK BELLY KUSHIYAKI

MAKES ABOUT 10 SKEWERS

DIFFICULTY

Not difficult at all

300 g (10½ oz) pork belly, rind removed
1 tablespoon salt
100 ml (3½ fl oz/scant ½ cup) sake
freshly ground black pepper, to serve

In the UK and America, we typically think of pork belly as something that has to be slow-cooked, roasted or braised for ages until the fat renders off and the meat falls apart. But even we have a fairly obvious exception to this: streaky bacon. Streaky bacon is still pork belly, after all, but the way it's sliced allows for quick, hot cooking. That's pretty much the idea behind Japanese pork belly skewers – the meat is sliced very thinly so that the fat renders and crisps over hot coals, while the meat itself stays juicy.

METHOD

Place the pork belly in the freezer for about half an hour – this will help firm it up so it's easier to slice. Using a very sharp knife, cut the pork belly into thin strips no more than 5 mm (¼ in) thick. (If your butcher has a deli slicer, ask if they can do this for you, and skip the freezer stage.)

Combine the salt and the sake, pour over the pork belly strips and leave to marinate for at least an hour and up to 24 hours in the fridge. Dry the strips on kitchen paper, cut them into bite-sized pieces and thread onto skewers. Wrap the ends of the skewers in foil and grill on very high, close to the heat, until the fatty bits go dark brown. Serve sprinkled with black pepper.

GRILLED MACKEREL, KABAYAKI STYLE

SERVES 4

DIFFICULTY

Divinely not difficult

Kabayaki is the most common way to prepare eel in Japan, in which the eel is filleted or butterflied, threaded onto thin skewers, soused in a sweet soy sauce glaze and grilled to a delightful crispy-soft texture. Eel, of course, is not the easiest fish to source in the UK, but this method works just as nicely with all manner of other oily, strong-flavoured fish, like sardines or mackerel.

2 whole mackerel, gutted
bunch of spring onions (scallions), cut in half
150 ml (5 fl oz/⅔ cup) Sweet Soy Sauce (page 173)
oil, for greasing
½ lemon, cut into wedges, to serve
sansho pepper or Shichimi Togarashi (page 180), to serve (optional)

METHOD

Score the mackerel on both sides with a sharp knife so that the glaze can penetrate the flesh. Lightly oil a baking tray and place the mackerel on it, with the spring onions on the side. Apply the sweet soy sauce to the surface of the fish liberally and place under a hot grill (broiler) on the highest rack. Re-glaze with the sauce every minute or so, and when the mackerel's skin is well browned (and blackened in places), carefully turn them over and repeat the process on the other side (if the spring onions are burning, remove them).

When that side is nicely coloured, check to see if the fish is cooked by looking inside its cavity – if the flesh nearest the spine has turned white or grey, it's done. Serve with a final coating of sweet soy sauce, lemon wedges and *sansho* pepper or shichimi, if you have it.

HIYAYAKKO

CHILLED TOFU WITH SOY SAUCE, GINGER AND KATSUOBUSHI

SERVES 2–4

DIFFICULTY

More an assembly job than an actual recipe, so very not difficult

- 1 block of firm silken tofu
- 4 tablespoons soy sauce
- 3 cm (1¼ in) piece of fresh ginger, peeled and finely grated
- 1 spring onion (scallion), finely sliced
- small handful of katsuobushi
- pinch of toasted sesame seeds

This dish does not read like something I'd particularly enjoy: cold tofu, doused in soy sauce, garnished with spring onions (scallions), grated ginger and katsuobushi tuna flakes. And yet it is so much more than the sum of its parts: moreish and satisfying but also light as a feather. It's lovely and refreshing in the summertime in particular, but really it's a dish for all seasons, and it could not be simpler to prepare.

METHOD

Cut the tofu into quarters, but keep it together for presentation. Place it in a shallow dish and pour over the soy sauce, then top with the ginger, spring onion, katsuobushi and sesame seeds.

BEEF TATAKI

SERVES 2–4

Tataki is a beautiful method of cooking: just seared, so you get the lovely, rich flavours of browned meat or fish, but still raw in the middle so you also get the most tender, juicy texture. It's the best of both worlds, and it's very, very, VERY easy. By the way, this recipe also works well with tuna, swordfish, salmon or any other kind of delicious, meaty fish you can get your hands on.

DIFFICULTY

Not at all difficult

- 60 ml (2 fl oz/¼ cup) sake
- 15 g (½ oz) caster (superfine) or granulated (raw) sugar
- 60 ml (2 fl oz/¼ cup) soy sauce
- 2 tablespoons oil
- 2 garlic cloves, finely sliced
- 300–350 g (10½–12 oz) steak, cut about 2.5 cm (1 in) thick – lean cuts free of sinew work best, so go for fillet, bavette or rump
- ¼ bunch of chives, finely sliced
- pinch of toasted sesame seeds
- handful of peppery leaves, like rocket or watercress
- 1 shallot, finely sliced and soaked in cold water

METHOD

Combine the sake and sugar in a small saucepan and bring to the boil. Remove from the heat and add the soy sauce. Leave to cool.

Put the oil in a sturdy frying pan (skillet) and add the garlic. Turn the heat to medium and let the garlic slowly brown. Remove the garlic when it's golden, and drain on kitchen paper. Crank the heat up on the pan – it should be stupidly, scarily, surface-of-the-sun hot. (It needs to be extremely hot to ensure the steak achieves a nice colour on the outside while remaining raw, or at least rare, in the middle.)

While the pan is coming up to temperature, dry the surface of your steak thoroughly with kitchen paper. Carefully lay your steak in the pan and let it develop a very rich, deep, dark brown colour. Turn the steak and let the other side colour as well. Remove from the pan and immediately transfer to the freezer.

Let the meat firm up in the freezer for about 20 minutes, then remove and slice it very thinly. Pour over the sake and soy mixture, and garnish with the fried garlic, chives and sesame seeds. Top with a handful of leaves and the drained shallot.

SALMON TATAKI WITH PONZU AND GREEN CHILLIES

SERVES 2–4

DIFFICULTY

Sooooooo
not difficult

sesame oil, for greasing
200 g (7 oz) salmon, pin-boned and skinned – if you can, get just the loin rather than the whole fillet
100 ml (3½ fl oz/scant ½ cup) Ponzu (page 176)
1 green chilli, very thinly sliced
2 teaspoons toasted sesame seeds
a few drops of chilli oil, to serve

I love the silky texture and fresh, sweet flavour of raw salmon, but of course I also love the dense, meaty flavour of grilled salmon – this delivers the best of both worlds, with tangy ponzu and hot green chillies to offset the richness of the fish.

METHOD

Lightly grease a baking tray with sesame oil and place the salmon on it. Grill under a very high heat until it begins to brown. Move the salmon around as needed to ensure an even colour. Turn over and repeat on the other side. Remove from the heat and leave to cool, then slice the salmon thinly and arrange on small plates. Pour over the ponzu and top with the green chilli and sesame seeds. Drizzle a tiny bit of chilli oil over the top.

SUSHI

3

寿司

Sushi! Japanese food's most popular gateway drug. When I tell people I cook Japanese food for a living, about 99 per cent of them respond: 'Ah! I love sushi!' (I don't have the heart to tell them my restaurant doesn't actually serve sushi – instead, I just smile and nod and bask in their radiant sushi love.) Many people seem very impressed with the imagined artistry of it all, but y'know what? It's actually pretty damn easy to make yourself.

HOW TO MAKE S U S H I WITH NO EXPERIENCE AND NO SPECIAL EQUIPMENT

Alright, so here's the deal with sushi: it is simple *in the extreme*. That means that there is nowhere to hide, and if you want to make delicious sushi, every element must be made as close to perfectly as possible. The rice must be cooked and seasoned *perfectly*. The fish must be selected and prepared *perfectly*. The wasabi and soy sauce must be judged *perfectly*.

That is... *if you run a sushi bar*. If you're just making sushi at home, who cares?! It just has to be delicious! Don't worry if it's not perfect. As long as the rice is nice, the fish is fresh and the seasonings are to your liking, then that's all that matters.

If you already have a sushi mat – probably collecting dust somewhere in the back of a drawer – then by all means use it. But if you don't have one, DON'T BUY ONE! You can make sushi just as easily with just a tea towel.

SUSHI RICE

MAKES ABOUT 600 G
(1 LB 5 OZ/3 CUPS)

DIFFICULTY

Maybe difficult if you want a Michelin star – but not if you just want some tasty sushi

Sushi rice is simply Japanese rice dressed with a seasoned vinegar, a practice now done mainly for flavour, but that has its roots in the need to preserve both the rice and the fish with acidity and salt in the days before refrigeration. It's subtle, but it adds an important element of seasoning that brings out the natural sweetness of both the rice and the fish.

300 g (10½ oz/1½ cups) Japanese rice, washed
390 g (13¾ oz/1⅔ cups) water
2 tablespoons rice vinegar – now is the time to bust out the NICE rice vinegar
2 tablespoons caster (superfine) or granulated (raw) sugar
1 tablespoon salt

METHOD

Cook the rice in the water, according to the instructions on page 19. While the rice is cooking, stir together the vinegar, sugar and salt until the sugar and salt dissolve.

Once the rice is cooked, spread it out in a large bowl or tray and sprinkle over the seasoned vinegar. Mix the vinegar through the rice with a rice paddle or spatula, using slicing and turning motions. Return the rice to the cooking pan or to a plastic container to keep it warm – for me, sushi is best when the rice is slightly above body temperature, so it's good to get all your sushi ingredients ready as the rice cooks, so it doesn't get too cold while you finish your prep.

An awful lot of recipes for sushi, or similar raw fish dishes, call for something called 'sashimi-grade' or 'sushi-grade' fish. The problem with this is... it doesn't actually exist. There is no such legal definition, no such supermarket category, no such fishmongers' labelling scheme – nothing! I've seen shops selling fish *clearly* unfit for raw consumption as 'sashimi-grade', and supermarkets selling perfectly fresh, safe fish with labels that warn us to 'ensure product is piping hot' before serving.

It's all nonsense. The bottom line is this: if you're eating fish raw, it has to A) be reasonably fresh, B) have been kept cold from the ocean to your fridge, and C) be handled and prepared hygienically from the boat all the way to your mouth. So who can you trust, given that most of this is out of your control? There are three sources you can turn to:

YOUR TRUSTED LOCAL FISHMONGER

Independent fishmongers typically know where their stock comes from, how it has been handled, and exactly how fresh it is – and it's in their own business interests to not sell any dicey fish. Explain to them that you need fish that's safe to eat raw and they're unlikely to let you down. And if you're not sure you can trust them, seek out their food hygiene rating on the internet.

YOUR NOT-SO-TRUSTED LOCAL SUPERMARKET

Big supermarkets are *obsessive* about food safety because slip-ups could cost them millions in wastage, fines and fees. Fish is kept cold and fresh from shore to shelf, and if it isn't, or if there's even a *possibility* that it isn't, then into the bin it goes. Not only that, but big supermarkets have a high turnover of stock, their packaging is clearly dated, and nowadays they also often provide information about providence and handling. Supermarket fish is actually a pretty safe bet for sushi. Just don't choose the stuff that's got one day left before its use-by date!

YOUR NOT-SO-VERY-LOCAL JAPANESE GROCER

Japanese supermarkets sell flash-frozen fish of all kinds specifically for sushi and sashimi – there is no question that they are safe to eat raw, and the quality is often excellent. However, this option tends to be very expensive, and not at all convenient if you don't live near a Japanese supermarket. You can order frozen fish for sashimi online as well, but that drives the price up even further. That said, there is something lovely about a piece of firm Japanese *hamachi* or buttery *otoro* – and for things like that, a splurge at the Japanese freezer section is the only option.

CHOOSING FISH

SPICY TUNA ROLL

MAKES 2 ROLLS

I chose this modern American sushi shop classic mainly to illustrate the technique of making *makizushi* – sushi rolls – because once you know it, you can fill them with pretty much anything. I like spicy tuna rolls because… well, because they're just delicious. Not exactly the pinnacle of sushi art, but they're probably the sushi I crave the most.

By the way, this is also *really* tasty with queenie scallops in place of tuna.

DIFFICULTY

Have you ever rolled up
a newspaper to swat a fly?
This is as not difficult as that
(the rolling bit, not the swatting bit)

- 100 g (3½ oz) fresh tuna, diced
- 2 spring onions (scallions), chopped
- 2 tablespoons mayonnaise
- 1 tablespoon sriracha or similar hot chilli sauce (or more or less, to taste)
- 1 teaspoon toasted sesame seeds
- 1 sheet of nori, cut in half lengthways
- 200 g (7 oz/scant 2 cups) prepared sushi rice (page 89)

METHOD

Stir together the tuna, spring onions, mayo, sriracha and sesame seeds.

Have a bowl of water handy – you will use this to wet your hands to keep the rice from sticking to your fingers. Lay the nori shiny side down on a dry, clean tea towel or cloth napkin. Rub your hands with water and shake off any excess, then use your fingers to spread the rice out in an even layer on the nori, leaving a gap of about 3 cm (1¼ in) uncovered along the far edge of the nori (you will use this to seal the roll).

Spread the spicy tuna mixture over the rice along the near edge, about 1 cm (½ in) from the edge. Now we roll. Use the tea towel to curl up the edge of the nori, over the filling, tightening the roll as you go with gentle pressure. When you've rolled to the far edge of the nori, use a little (just a little) water on your fingers to dampen the exposed nori, and press the roll together to seal. With a little luck you'll have a tight, structurally sound spicy tuna roll – slice with a sharp, wet knife, and enjoy with typical sushi accoutrements.

SALMON, AVOCADO AND CUCUMBER ROLL

MAKES 2 ROLLS

It's like a sandwich, in sushi form. Meaty salmon, buttery avocado, crisp cucumber – what's not to love?

METHOD

Proceed with the instructions for spicy tuna rolls opposite, but with the salmon, avocado, cucumber and wasabi in place of the spicy tuna mix.

DIFFICULTY

Shamefully not difficult

1 sheet of nori, cut in half lengthways
200 g (7 oz/scant 2 cups) prepared sushi rice (page 89)
100 g (3½ oz) salmon, pin-boned and skinned, cut into strips 1 cm (½ in) thick
½ avocado, cut into strips 5 mm (¼ in) thick and tossed with the juice of ½ lemon
¼ cucumber, cut into batons 5 mm (¼ in) thick
wasabi, to taste

SHIMESABA OSHIZUSHI

CURED MACKEREL PRESSED SUSHI

MAKES 12–16 PIECES OF SUSHI

DIFFICULTY

Impressively not difficult

We've covered sushi rolls, but what about *nigiri* sushi – the more traditional, altogether more delicate preparation of fish on a pillow of rice? That's something that actually does take practice. However, there's a somewhat obscure type of sushi that can approximate the format of nigiri without the need to apprentice in Tokyo for four years – it's called *oshizushi*, or pressed sushi. Essentially, prepared fish is placed on top of a bed of sushi rice, and then the whole thing is gently pressed. The fish adheres to the rice, which is then sliced into nigiri-like bite-sized pieces. I chose pickled mackerel, but the same technique can be applied to any fish.

salt
2 mackerel fillets, pin-boned and cleaned of any traces of blood
150 ml (5 fl oz/⅔ cup) vinegar
1 small piece of kombu, about 5 cm (2 in) square, briefly soaked in cold water to soften (optional)
240 g (8½ oz/2 cups) prepared sushi rice (page 89)
wasabi, to taste
soy sauce, to serve

METHOD

You will need a small, rectangular container for this, along with a plate, another container, or just a piece of cardboard wrapped in cling film (plastic wrap) that fits snugly inside that container.

Rub a liberal amount of salt into both sides of the mackerel fillets. Leave to cure in the fridge for at least 2 hours and up to 4, then rinse off the salt and pat dry with kitchen paper. Transfer to a ziplock bag or container, pour in the vinegar and add the kombu, if using. Seal and leave to pickle in the fridge for another 2 hours and up to 8 hours, then remove the fish, pat dry and gently peel off its transparent skin (it should be slightly loose at the head end).

Line your container with cling film and pack the rice into it in an even layer. Spread a little wasabi on top of the rice and lay the mackerel fillets on top, head-to-tail, so they cover as much of the rice as possible. Set your plate/container/cardboard on top and press down firmly so everything compresses and sticks together. Use the cling film to remove the rice and fish from the container. Remove the cling film, then slice down the centre, between the two fillets. Cut each half into bite-sized pieces of sushi and enjoy with soy sauce.

BIG DISHES

4

メインディッシュ

These recipes are meant for sharing – big, generous platters/plates/bowls/dishes/pots/pans/trays/slabs of hot, hearty food to be enjoyed with family and friends (or just whoever is in the vicinity and loves Japanese food). Some of it is even cooked communally, which makes dinner that much easier and more fun. As with the small dishes, these are typically accompanied by a side or two, such as rice, miso soup, pickles or salad. But some of them are perfectly satisfying on their own.

TEMPURA

SERVES 4

Tempura is a fantastic place to start on a journey into the world of Japanese food, because it's so simple, such a crowd-pleaser, and it requires no special ingredients. If you're put off by the idea of deep-frying, let me put some of your fears to rest. First of all, it's not as unhealthy as you might think – if you measure your oil before and after making a tempura meal, you'll find you won't have actually used that much. It's also not unsafe, provided you use common sense and a very big pan. Finally, it's not difficult – simply dip, drop and drain.

DIFFICULTY

Not at all difficult

oil, for deep-frying – about 1.5 litres (51 fl oz/6 cups) but possibly a little more depending on the size of your pan
8 broccoli florets or Tenderstem broccoli stems
1 large or 2 small onions, cut into 7.5 mm (⅓ in) rounds
8 oyster mushrooms
1 courgette (zucchini), cut in half and then into quarters lengthways
8 king prawns (shrimp), peeled and deveined, scored 5–6 times on their underside to prevent them from curling
200 g (7 oz) skinless, boneless cod or other meaty white fish, cut into 4 goujons
400 ml (13 fl oz/ generous 1½ cups) Tsuyu (page 176), to serve (optional – you can season this with just salt and a wedge of lemon if you like)

For the batter
1 egg
400 ml (13 fl oz/generous 1½ cups) sparkling water
200 g (7 oz/1½ cups) plain (all-purpose) flour
100 g (3½ oz/1 cup) cornflour (cornstarch)
pinch of salt

METHOD

Get all your ingredients ready to go before cooking – bear in mind that this is quick, hot cooking, so anything cut too thick will risk burning before it cooks through. Pour the oil into a very big, deep pan, ensuring that you keep the oil level at least 7.5 cm (3 in) below the rim of the pan, to be safe. Put the oil over a medium heat while you make the batter.

For the batter, beat the egg, and then stir it together with the sparkling water, ideally using chopsticks. Don't stir too much or you will knock the bubbles out of the water.

Stir both flours together with the salt in a separate bowl, then pour in the egg and sparkling water mixture. Mix until the batter comes together with a consistency of double (heavy) cream. A general rule to follow is that it should be badly mixed: a slightly lumpy batter contains more air and irregularities that will give your tempura a light, lacy structure, and it also develops less gluten, which helps prevent it from turning doughy and soft. Little lumps are good, big lumps are bad, so break them up.

Now all you need to do before you start cooking is to check the temperature of the oil. If you have a thermometer, use it – the oil should be at 170–180°C (340–350°F). Or simply drip a few drops of the batter into the oil to test it. If the batter sinks, it's too cold. If the batter immediately floats and sizzles, it's too hot. The batter should sink just below the surface of the oil, then rise up and start to sizzle. Then it's just right.

Dunk the veg and fish in the batter, one at a time, allowing excess to drip off before carefully placing them in the oil. Use tongs or chopsticks to separate the veg as they fry so they don't stick together. You'll have to do the veg in batches – the ideal way to serve and eat this is straight out of the fryer, so if you've got somewhere for people to sit in the kitchen, gather them round for a TEMPURA PARTY!!! (Give people some pickles or the Best Edamame (page 27) to snack on while they wait between batches.) If not, just keep the tempura in a very low oven with the door slightly ajar to let out moisture until it's all ready to serve.

The tempura is done when it is a light golden brown and hard to the touch – use tongs or chopsticks to feel if the batter has firmed up before removing from the oil and draining on kitchen paper. Serve the tempura with tsuyu for dipping, or simply wedges of lemon and sea salt.

WHOLE GRILLED FISH WITH TSUYU AND GRATED RADISH

SERVES 2–4

DIFFICULTY

Beyond
not difficult

Apart from the occasional vast sushi platter, there aren't too many grand centrepiece dishes in Japanese cuisine – things tend to be more miniaturised. However, at parties and banquets sometimes guests will be presented with a gorgeous whole grilled fish, lightly seasoned with tsuyu and garnished with grated radish. It's very Japanese in that haiku/zen/wabi-sabi way – impressive and beautiful in its rustic simplicity.

- sea salt
- 1 big fish (any fish will do, really, but I like a flatfish like plaice, sole or brill), cleaned and scaled
- oil, for greasing
- 200–300 ml (scant 1–1¼ cups) Tsuyu (page 176), depending on the size of the fish
- about ¼ daikon radish or about 10 radishes, finely grated

METHOD

Sprinkle sea salt onto both sides of the fish and gently rub it into the skin. Leave it to sit for about an hour, so the salt penetrates the flesh. Place the fish on a lightly oiled baking tray and set under a hot grill. If your fish is quite thick, set it on a rack about 7 cm (2¾ in) away from the grill; if it's thin, set it on the uppermost rack. Grill on one side until the flesh has firmed up and the skin has begun to colour, then carefully turn over and repeat for the other side. The fish is cooked when the meat pulls easily from the bone.

Warm the tsuyu in a saucepan or the microwave. To serve, either give everybody their own bowl of tsuyu and a pile of grated radish, so they can dip their fish as they eat it, or you can simply mix the radish into the tsuyu and pour everything over the fish.

SWEET MISO-GRILLED COD

SERVES 4

This is a beautifully simple recipe, made famous by Nobu Matsuhisa and his global empire of restaurants. The only catch is that Nobu's version uses the hard-to-come-by black cod, which has a richer, more buttery flavour than your ordinary cod. But regular cod still works, and the recipe also works with similarly meaty fish like salmon, swordfish and (my favourite) Arctic char, if you can get it.

METHOD

Marinate the fish in the miso sauce for at least 30 minutes. For best results, leave overnight in the fridge, and for up to 3 days.

Line a baking tray with foil and rub it with a little oil. Set the rack about 10 cm (4 in) from the grill (broiler), and grill the cod for about 10 minutes on each side, until richly caramelised (a little bit of black is okay – but not too much, so keep your eye on it). If your cod is blackening too quickly, either lower the rack or shield the fish with a sheet of foil. The fish is cooked when it starts to feel firm and flakes easily – remember, if you undercook your fish, you can fix it, but if you overcook it, there's no going back. Always err on the side of rare! Serve with pickles, if you like.

DIFFICULTY

So not difficult you will wonder how Nobu gets away with charging so much for it

4 big fat cod fillets (or black cod, salmon, char, etc.)
180 ml (6½ fl oz/¾ cup) Sweet Miso Sauce (page 175)
oil, for greasing
Japanese Quick Pickles (page 30), to serve (optional)

SUKIYAKI

SUKIYAKI PARTY!!!

SERVES 2–4

Sukiyaki is one of those Japanese foods that's so fun and so easy I always wonder why it hasn't become more popular. Essentially, it's a sweet soy-based beef and vegetable hotpot. But like most Japanese hotpot dishes, the cooking is typically communal, done at the table. Prepared raw meat and vegetables are laid out alongside a bubbling cauldron of delicious broth-sauce, for diners to dunk in and cook to their liking, before retrieving it and immersing it in a bowl of dipping sauce on the side, and gobbling it up, piping hot. It's a joyous, convivial, exciting experience, and it's SUPER easy.

DIFFICULTY

Not at all difficult; in fact, you don't even have to do most of the cooking!

3 leeks, washed and trimmed, cut on the bias into slices 2 cm (¾ in) thick
500 g (1 lb 2 oz) turnips or daikon (mooli), peeled and cut into rounds 1 cm (½ in) thick
4 carrots, peeled and cut on the bias into slices 1 cm (½ in) thick
100 g (3½ oz) mangetout (snow peas)
½ hispi, Chinese or flat cabbage, cut into chunks 2–3 cm (¾–1¼ in) wide
200 g (7 oz) rocket (arugula), watercress or other peppery greens – keep an eye out for chrysanthemum greens (*tong ho* in Chinese) – they're amazing
300 g (10½ oz) mixed mushrooms – some supermarkets have an 'exotic' variety pack, or go for oyster or shiitake
800 g (1 lb 12 oz) bavette/flank steak, partially frozen and sliced very thinly against the grain
500 ml (17 fl oz/2 cups) Sesame Sauce (page 183) or 400 ml (13 fl oz/generous 1½ cups) Ponzu (page 176), for dipping
4 portions of noodles – fresh is best (ramen or udon)

For the broth-sauce
1 tablespoon oil
30 g (1 oz) dark brown sugar
500 ml (17 fl oz/2 cups) water, plus more as needed to top up
150 ml (5 fl oz/⅔ cup) sake
150 ml (5 fl oz/⅔ cup) soy sauce
10–15 g (⅓–½ oz) kombu, or 1 teaspoon dashi powder, or ½ beef stock cube (optional)

– If you're going to cook this at the table, you'll need a portable gas burner or some sort of electric cooker – induction or an ordinary ceramic one will be fine (just be careful of the cord).

METHOD

Prepare your veg and beef as described (and feel free to use different kinds, as well). Lay them all out beautifully on a bamboo platter hand-crafted by Shinto priests, or whatever large plate you have. Lay out the beef on a separate dish, and gather everyone around the table with the burner in the middle. Give everybody a bowl with some sesame sauce or ponzu in it.

Place a large hotpot or casserole on the burner, and add the oil. Add the brown sugar and let it melt and bubble, then add the water, sake, soy sauce and kombu/dashi powder/stock cube, if using. Bring this mixture to the boil and discard the kombu. Reduce the heat to a low boil/high simmer. Now we start cooking!

Pass around the meat and veg, allowing everyone to dip whatever they like into the broth and cook it to their liking – then they just fetch it out with chopsticks, dip in their dip, and eat! Over time the broth will take on the flavour of everything that goes into it, becoming rich and deep. It will also reduce – top up with water as needed to keep the party going.

Once the veg and meat have been devoured, bust out the noodles. At this time you should stop topping up the broth and let it reduce into a luscious, sweet sauce. Add the noodles and cook them until tender, then slurp them up (the dipping sauce will probably be gone at this point, but you won't need it anymore because of how much flavour and substance you get from the broth itself).

It's really a tremendously fun and fortifying meal, especially nice for a dinner party in winter. But you can do it as an ordinary weekday dinner, too, and without the portable burner. Just make the broth as stated above, then cook all the veg to your liking, and add the meat and noodles last. Ladle it out into big, deep bowls as a kind of sukiyaki stew – oh, and you won't need the dipping sauce if you cook it this way, but a little bit of lemon is nice to offset the rich sweetness of the broth.

CHANKO NABE

SUMO HOTPOT

SERVES 4 – POSSIBLY MORE

This light yet extremely filling hotpot dish is famous for being a key part of the weight-gain diet of sumo wrestlers. Indeed, what distinguishes it isn't any particular flavour or ingredients – it can be made from just about anything – but its *volume*. So whatever you choose to put in it, just make sure you choose a *lot* of it. That's the whole point! Like Sukiyaki (opposite) or other Japanese hotpots, this dish is more fun and easier if it's cooked communally, at the table. But you can do it all together in the kitchen as well – totally up to you.

DIFFICULTY

The only difficult part is rolling away from the table after you've eaten as much as a trainee sumo wrestler

- 1 litre (34 fl oz/4 cups) chicken stock, dashi, or a mix of both
- 100 ml (3½ fl oz/scant ½ cup) sake
- 100 ml (3½ fl oz/scant ½ cup) mirin
- 100 ml (3½ fl oz/scant ½ cup) soy sauce
- 4 portions of cooked rice (300 g/ 10½ oz/1½ cups uncooked)
- 150–180 ml (5–6½ fl oz/⅔–¾ cup) soy sauce or Ponzu (page 176)
- ½ Chinese leaf (Napa cabbage), cut into chunks
- 400–600 g (14 oz–1 lb 6 oz) firm tofu, cut into large blocks
- 200–300 g (7–10½ oz) mushrooms – I recommend enoki, shimeji/ beech, shiitake and/or oyster
- 2 bok choi, quartered, or 4 baby bok choi, halved
- ½ daikon, peeled and cut into rounds, or 200–300 g (7–10½ oz) turnips, peeled and quartered
- 4 chicken thighs, boneless, cut into bite-sized pieces
- 150–200 g (5–7 oz) raw king prawns (shrimp), shelled and deveined
- 4 portions of ramen, udon or *shirataki* noodles (optional)

METHOD

Place a large pot or flameproof casserole on a burner in the centre of the table and pour in the stock/dashi, sake, mirin and soy sauce. Give everybody a bowl of rice and a little dish of ponzu or soy sauce. Have your vegetables prepped and ready to go on a platter, and your raw meat and shellfish ready on a separate platter (remember to use separate tongs or chopsticks for handling the raw meat). Once the broth is simmering, start cooking!

Pass around the meat, shellfish and veg, allowing everyone to drop whatever they fancy into the broth and cook it to their liking – then rescue it with chopsticks, dip it in ponzu or soy sauce, and eat! Over time the broth become rich and deep as it takes on the flavour of the ingredients. It will also reduce – top up with water as needed. If you like, once all the meat and veg have been devoured, let the broth reduce and add noodles. Once they're cooked, remove from the heat and slurp them up along with the broth.

Repeat frequently to make your sumo-wrestling dreams come true.

NIKUJAGA

JAPANESE BEEF AND POTATO STEW

SERVES 4

DIFFICULTY

Not at all difficult

250–300 g (9–10½ oz) beef rump, skirt or fillet
2 carrots, peeled
2 large baking potatoes, peeled
1 large or 2 small onions, peeled
1 leek, washed and trimmed
1 tablespoon vegetable oil
200 g (7 oz) mangetout (snow peas)
500 ml (17 fl oz/2 cups) dashi or beef stock, or a mix of both
50 ml (2 fl oz) mirin
50 ml (2 fl oz) soy sauce
1 tablespoon Worcestershire sauce or Tonkatsu Sauce (page 182)
1 tablespoon sake
1 tablespoon caster (superfine) or granulated (raw) sugar
4 portions of cooked rice (300 g/10½ oz/1½ cups uncooked) or noodles

This comfort food classic has the best name when translated literally: 'meat potato'. It's Japan's answer to a beef and potato stew, but it has a light dashi and soy-based broth rather than a thick gravy. It's hearty and satisfying but not too heavy – oh, and it's much easier to make (and spell) than a traditional boeuf bourgihguinognuon (?!?!).

METHOD

Put the beef in the freezer for 30–45 minutes to firm up, then slice it across the grain as thinly as possible. Cut the carrots and potatoes into wedges, thinly slice the onion/s and cut the leek on the bias into 4 pieces.

Heat the oil in a deep pan or flameproof casserole over a medium heat, add the onion and fry until just starting to soften, then add all the vegetables except the mangetout. Add the dashi and/or stock, the mirin, soy sauce, Worcestershire or tonkatsu sauce, sake and sugar. Bring to a high simmer, then cover with a circle of baking parchment or lid and continue to simmer for about 10–15 minutes, until all the vegetables are tender. Add the mangetout and cook for just another minute, then remove from the heat and add the beef – since it is so thin, it will cook in the hot broth. Skim any scum off the top with a ladle or a small sieve. Serve over noodles or with rice on the side.

BUTA SHOGAYAKI

STIR-FRIED PORK WITH GINGER SAUCE

SERVES 4

I remember having this for lunch a lot in Japan, but it's just as nice for dinner – and it's very, very fast to prepare. The ginger sauce, by the way, works well in other dishes as well. Try it as a marinade for chicken or a glaze for fish.

METHOD

Cut the pork belly in half lengthways and place in the freezer for 30–45 minutes to firm up, then slice it very thinly. Purée the ginger with the soy sauce, mirin, sake, ketchup and sesame oil in a blender or food processor. If you don't have a food processor, simply finely grate the ginger and stir together with the other ingredients.

Heat the vegetable oil in a wok or deep frying pan (skillet) and add the pork and cabbage. Stir-fry for 3–4 minutes, then add the bean sprouts and the ginger sauce. Keep stir-frying until the sprouts have softened slightly and the sauce has coated everything nicely. Top with the spring onions and garnish with sesame seeds. Serve with rice.

DIFFICULTY

Definitely not difficult

400 g (14 oz) pork belly, rind removed
60 g (2 oz) fresh ginger, peeled and thinly sliced against the grain
6 tablespoons soy sauce
6 tablespoons mirin
4 tablespoons sake
1 tablespoon ketchup
1 teaspoon sesame oil
1 tablespoon vegetable oil
½ hispi (pointed) cabbage, shredded
150 g (5 oz) bean sprouts
2 spring onions (scallions), finely sliced
toasted sesame seeds, to garnish

BUTA KAKUNI

SWEET SOY AND STOUT-BRAISED PORK BELLY

SERVES 4

This recipe is perhaps more Chinese than Japanese, but it's common in both casual Japanese restaurants and home kitchens. I don't want to say it's the best pork belly ever… but I guess I just did. If the addition of stout sounds strange, consider it has some of the same treacly-savoury flavour as soy sauce, but without the salt.

DIFFICULTY

Completely not difficult

- 2 tablespoons vegetable oil
- 500 g (1 lb 2 oz) pork belly, rind removed, cut into cubes
- 1 onion, peeled and cut into quarters
- 1 whole garlic bulb, cut in half around its middle
- 300 ml (10 fl oz/1¼ cups) stout
- 100 ml (3½ oz/scant ½ cup) dashi
- 4 tablespoons dark brown sugar
- 4 tablespoons mirin
- 4 tablespoons soy sauce
- 4 star anise
- 1 cinnamon stick, 4–5 cm (1½–2 in)
- water, as needed

METHOD

Preheat the oven to 130°C (275°F/Gas 1).

Put the oil in a deep flameproof casserole and set it over a medium-high heat. When the oil is very hot, add the pork belly and brown on all sides. Remove the meat and drain excess oil from the pan, then add the onion and garlic and brown them all over. Pour in the stout, dashi, sugar, mirin and soy sauce, and add the star anise and cinnamon. Bring to the boil, then reduce the heat and add the pork belly. If the liquid does not cover the meat, add water.

Place a circle of baking parchment or foil over the meat, put a lid on the casserole and place in the preheated oven. This will take probably 4–5 hours to braise, but start checking it after 2 hours. If the liquid is reducing too much, top it up and turn the oven heat down – the liquid should be at a bare simmer. The pork is done when it is very, very soft. Remove it carefully with a slotted spoon, then pass the braising liquid through a sieve into another saucepan. Skim as much fat off the surface of the sauce as possible, then bring to the boil and reduce to the consistency of thin syrup. Pour the sauce over the pork before serving. Enjoy with rice or noodles, and savoury green vegetables such as broccoli or bok choi.

TONKATSU

JAPANESE PORK CUTLET

SERVES 2–4

DIFFICULTY

The most difficult part is resisting the urge to eat this every day

Most of the recipes in this book are quite traditional, but I couldn't resist doing something a little different for this one.

Tonkatsu is essentially Japan's take on schnitzel – a breaded and fried pork cutlet. Most tonkatsu, and indeed most schnitzel, is tasty, but rarely as amazing as deep-fried pork really ought to be. I reckon this is because most tonkatsu use a very thin piece of pork, which dries out before the breadcrumbs develop a really rich colour and flavour. So when I was developing a tonkatsu dish for the restaurant, it occurred to me that conventional wisdom had it wrong on this one: the pork should be *thick*, not thin and, even better, it should be cooked on the bone. The thick cut keeps the pork juicy as the outside browns and crisps, while the bone contributes flavour and additional moisture.

- 2 big, thick pork chops, bone in and rind removed
- sea salt and freshly ground black pepper
- plain (all-purpose) flour, for dredging
- 2 eggs, beaten with a splash of water or milk
- 150–200 g (5–7 oz/3½–4½ cups) panko breadcrumbs
- oil, for deep-frying
- ½ hispi (pointed) cabbage, very finely shredded
- ½ lemon (optional)
- 150 ml (5 fl oz/⅔ cup) Tonkatsu Sauce (page 182)

METHOD

Season the pork chops liberally with salt and pepper; ideally you should do this about an hour ahead of cooking, so the seasoning can penetrate the pork. But no worries if not. Dredge the chops in flour, then soak them in the beaten egg, then coat them in panko.

Pour enough oil into a large, deep pan (the widest you have) to come no more than halfway up the sides. If your pan is not wide enough to fit both chops, you may have to fry them in batches. Heat to 160°C (320°F) and gently lower the chops into the oil. It will take at least 10 minutes for them to cook through – keep an eye on them and turn them once during cooking. The best way to check if they are done is to use a meat thermometer – I prefer these well done, so an internal temperature of 60°C (140°F) at the thickest point is good for me. But some people like their pork a little more pink, so go for 57–58°C (134–136°F), or for VERY well done, aim for 65°C (149°F). If you don't have a thermometer, you're going to have to do some exploratory surgery. Find the bone, and cut alongside it to check (but bear in mind the meat nearest the bone will still be pinkish even when it's well done). If the meat's not cooked through but the breadcrumbs are getting too dark, place the chops on a wire rack in an oven set to 180°C (350°F/Gas 4) for another 10 minutes or so. If the breadcrumbs are still light in colour, just put the chops back in the oil for a few minutes.

Drain the chops on a wire rack or kitchen paper and rest them for at least 5 minutes before carving. Cut along the bone with a thin knife, then slice across the meat into thin, chopstick-friendly pieces. Garnish with plenty of sea salt and serve with shredded cabbage, lemon, if you like, and tonkatsu sauce on the side. Also, these are brilliant with a fried egg on top!

HAMBAGU

JAPANESE STEAK HACHÉ

SERVES 4

The steak haché, or hamburger steak, is something that's long fallen out of fashion in Europe and America, but in Japan it's still common at casual restaurants. There are even whole chains specialising in them, one of which has perhaps my favourite name of any restaurant anywhere: Bikkuri Donkey (translation: Surprise Donkey). The hamburger steak is thoroughly, undeniably lowbrow, it's true, but it's also very good, especially done the Japanese way – with a sweet dashi-soy sauce and tons of onions worked through the mince for moisture and flavour.

METHOD

Combine the breadcrumbs, parsley, onions, garlic and some salt and pepper in a food processor until a coarse paste is formed. Mix this into the beef mince and form into 4 patties.

Combine the sweet soy sauce, dashi, ketchup and Worcestershire sauce in a saucepan and bring to the boil. Set a frying pan (skillet) or griddle over a very high heat and fry the beef patties in a little of the oil for about 3–5 minutes on each side, or longer for well done.

Meanwhile, heat the remaining oil in a separate frying pan and fry the eggs. When the burgers are nearly done, pour over the sweet soy sauce mixture and top each with a slice of cheese. Place the burgers under a hot grill until the cheese melts and browns slightly, then remove and top each burger with a fried egg. Serve with the sauce poured on the side, sprinkled with the crispy fried onions. Add parsley to garnish. In Japan this is typically served with rice and a salad, but I like it with mash or chips.

DIFFICULTY

Not difficult

- 80 g (3 oz/1½ cups) breadcrumbs
- 10–12 flat-leaf parsley sprigs, plus a few extra leaves, chopped, to garnish
- 1 large or 2 small onions, roughly chopped
- 2 garlic cloves, peeled
- salt and freshly ground black pepper
- 600 g (1 lb 5 oz) beef mince (ground beef) – try to get a fairly coarse, fatty mince
- 200 ml (7 fl oz/scant 1 cup) Sweet Soy Sauce (page 173)
- 100 ml (3½ fl oz/scant ½ cup) dashi
- 2 tablespoons ketchup
- 1 tablespoon Worcestershire sauce
- 1 tablespoon vegetable oil
- 4 eggs
- 4 slices of Gruyère, 100 g (3½ oz) in total
- 100 g (3½ oz) crispy fried onions

BIG RICE &

5

ご飯物と麺類

These dishes are based on rice or noodles, so unlike the recipes in the preceding chapters, they make for a good, filling meal on their own. But feel free to add a few sides for a proper Japanese feast!

NOODLE DISHES

JAPANESE CARBONARA

SERVES 4

DIFFICULTY

It's pasta!
Therefore, not difficult

Believe it or not, there is a whole world of Japanese pasta dishes, collectively known as *wafu* (Japanese-style) pasta. Almost invariably based on spaghetti (which is not so different from ramen, in a way), Japanese pasta often resembles traditional Italian or Italian-American pasta dishes, but with innovative touches based on indigenous Japanese flavours. A classic example is *mentaiko* pasta, which uses pollock roe cured with chilli to flavour a buttery sauce – the flavour of mentaiko is kind of like a combination of Italian *bottarga* and chilli, so it makes sense.

There aren't really any rules when it comes to Japanese pasta, so feel free to play around with this. It is remarkable how well most Japanese flavours work stirred through spaghetti.

- 50 g (2 oz/3½ tablespoons) butter
- 1 onion, finely chopped
- 200 g (7 oz) oyster or shiitake mushrooms (stems removed), thinly sliced
- 4 garlic cloves, grated or very finely chopped
- 2 tablespoons sake
- a few pinches of freshly ground black pepper
- 4 tablespoons miso
- 4 tablespoons dashi
- 2 eggs, beaten
- juice of ½ lemon
- 500 g (1 lb 2 oz) dried spaghetti
- salt
- toasted sesame seeds
- ½ sheet nori, cut into fine shreds with scissors
- 25–30 g (¾ oz–1 oz) Parmesan or pecorino
- 2 spring onions (scallions), finely sliced
- 60 g (2 oz) ikura (salmon roe), optional

METHOD

Melt the butter in a large frying pan (skillet) and add the onion and mushrooms. Fry until the onion and mushrooms are just golden brown, then add the garlic and cook until soft. Add the sake and black pepper and stir through. Reduce the heat to low.

In a bowl, whisk together the miso, dashi, eggs and lemon juice, ensuring that no lumps of miso remain.

Cook the pasta at a rolling boil to your liking, then drain well and return to the pan. Add the onions and mushrooms and the miso-egg mixture, and stir through – be quick with this, so the residual heat from the pasta cooks the eggs and thickens the sauce. Taste and adjust the seasoning with salt as needed. Garnish with sesame seeds, the shredded nori, Parmesan and chives, and a nice dollop of *ikura*, if using, in the middle.

KARE RAISU

CURRY RICE

SERVES 2–4

The story of Japanese curry is one of global empires rising and falling. Before the end of the 19th century, there was no curry in Japan. It was introduced not from India, Bangladesh, Thailand, Malaysia or anywhere else that can be thought of as somewhere curry originates – but from Britain. At that time, South Asian curry had already been integrated into the imperial diet, and it was British military officers and diplomats who introduced it to the Japanese. British curry – not very spicy, thickened with flour – caught on, particularly within the Japanese navy and army, where it was celebrated as an economical and tasty way to feed hundreds of hungry servicemen.

Curry remains one of Japan's favourite comfort foods, delicious as it is weirdly divorced from curry's Asian origins. Whereas an Indian curry will be naturally thick from puréed onions/tomatoes/chillies and a whole heap of spices, Japan's curry is based on a flour-and-butter roux that thickens a lightly-spiced stock-based sauce. I do love Japanese curry, but I also love South Asian curries with their vibrancy and layers of flavour. This recipe combines the two. I keep it vegetarian, because I find it just as satisfying that way, but if you want you can add chicken, beef or pork to this. In fact, you can add just about anything you want (at the restaurant we put ham and cheese on it and it's amazing).

(Note: if you want a really authentic and REALLY easy Japanese curry experience at home, just buy a box of instant Japanese curry at the Asian supermarket. No, really – it's good and cheap and fast, and it really doesn't get much more authentic than that!)

METHOD

For the sauce, combine the oil, onion, ginger, chilli, garlic, tomatoes, apple, banana, curry powder and garam masala in a food processor and blitz to a paste. Pour this into a saucepan and cook on a medium-high heat, stirring often, until the mixture begins to caramelise and the spices become aromatic. Add the stock and bring to the boil.

Meanwhile, melt the butter in a separate saucepan and whisk in the flour. Cook on a low heat for about 8 minutes, stirring constantly, until the roux thickens and turns a golden brown colour. Ladle the curry mixture from the other pan into the roux, a little at a time, whisking constantly to incorporate. Add the ketchup and soy sauce. Cook the mixture until it's quite thick, then transfer to a blender or use an immersion blender to purée until very smooth. Taste and adjust the seasoning with salt.

Place the onion, carrots and potatoes in a saucepan and cover with water. Bring to the boil, add the cauliflower and reduce to a simmer. Cook for about 10 minutes, until everything is tender. Drain and return to the pan, and pour in the curry sauce. Bring everything back to a simmer and serve with the rice.

DIFFICULTY

Probably the least difficult curry you'll ever make

1 onion, cut into small chunks
2 carrots, peeled and cut into wedges
400 g (14 oz) floury potatoes, peeled and cut into bite-sized chunks
½ cauliflower, broken into bite-sized florets
4 portions of cooked rice (300 g/10½ oz/1½ cups uncooked)

For the curry sauce
4 tablespoons oil
1 large onion, roughly chopped
2 cm (¾ in) piece of fresh ginger, peeled and finely sliced
1 green chilli, roughly chopped
2 garlic cloves, peeled
2 tomatoes
½ Golden Delicious or similar apple, peeled and roughly chopped
½ banana
30 g (1 oz) mild Madras curry powder
2 tablespoons garam masala
750 ml (25 fl oz/3 cups) chicken or beef stock
60 g (2 oz/½ stick) butter
6 tablespoons plain (all-purpose) flour
2 tablespoons ketchup
2 tablespoons soy sauce
salt

KATSU KARE

KATSU CURRY

SERVES 4

Katsu curry is simply Japanese curry rice with the delightful addition of breaded, fried meat, typically chicken. The recipe is exactly the same as it is for Curry Rice (page 128), plus the katsu below. Feel free to use less veg if you like, since there will be more bulk provided by the katsu.

DIFFICULTY

So not difficult you will never order this at a restaurant again

1 quantity Curry Rice (page 128)
2 skinless, boneless chicken breasts, cut in half horizontally to produce two thin escalopes
salt and freshly ground black pepper
plain (all-purpose) flour, for dredging
1 egg, beaten with a splash of milk or water
200 g (7 oz/4⅔ cups) panko breadcrumbs
oil, for shallow-frying

METHOD

Season the chicken breasts well with salt and pepper, then dredge in flour. Soak them in the beaten egg, then coat them thoroughly with the panko.

Heat a little oil (about a 2 mm/1⁄16 in depth) in a large frying pan (skillet) over a medium heat. Lay the breaded chicken in the oil and cook for 5–6 minutes on each side. Remove and drain on kitchen paper or a wire rack. Leave to rest briefly before slicing and serving atop the curry rice.

OYAKODON

CHICKEN AND EGG RICE BOWL

SERVES 4

DIFFICULTY

Super
not difficult

80 g (3 oz/¾ stick) butter
2 onions, thinly sliced
4 skinless, boneless chicken thighs, cut into bite-sized pieces
100 g (3½ oz) shiitake mushrooms, de-stemmed and thinly sliced
200 ml (7 fl oz/scant 1 cup) dashi
3 tablespoons soy sauce
2 tablespoons mirin
1 tablespoon caster (superfine) or granulated (raw) sugar
8 eggs
4 large portions of cooked rice (350-400 g/12–14 oz/ 1¾–2 cups uncooked)
2 spring onions (scallions), sliced
pinch of Shichimi Togarashi (page 180), to serve (optional)

This comforting recipe has a name that's kinda cute, kinda disturbing if you translate it directly: 'parent and child' rice bowl. Which I suppose, at the very least, is a little more poetic than 'chicken and egg'. At any rate, it's VERY delicious. It doesn't usually contain butter or mushrooms but for me the combination of butter, eggs, mushrooms and sweet soy is irresistible.

METHOD

Melt the butter in a large frying pan (skillet) over a medium heat, then add the onions. Cook until the onions soften and brown, being careful to avoid burning the butter. Add the chicken thighs and mushrooms and cook until these begin to brown as well, stirring frequently.

Pour in the dashi, soy sauce, mirin and sugar and let it reduce slightly, coating the chicken. Reduce the heat to low and crack in the eggs. Break up the yolks and stir the eggs gently a few times; you should keep them very loose and runny, almost like a sauce for the chicken and rice. When the eggs are cooked to a semi-scrambled consistency, remove from the heat.

Scoop the rice into deep bowls and spoon over the chicken and egg mixture. Garnish with the spring onions and the shichimi, if you like.

GYUDON

BEEF, ONION AND SWEET SOY RICE BOWL

SERVES 4

DIFFICULTY

Not difficult at all

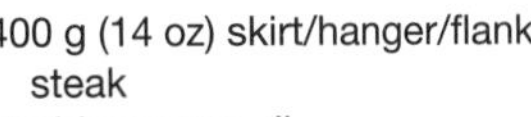

400 g (14 oz) skirt/hanger/flank steak
2 tablespoons oil
4 onions, thinly sliced
2 cm (¾ in) piece of fresh ginger, peeled and finely julienned
200 ml (7 fl oz/scant 1 cup) Sweet Soy Sauce (page 173)
100 ml (3½ fl oz/scant ½ cup) dashi
4 large portions of cooked rice (350–400 g/12–14 oz/ 1¾–2 cups uncooked)
40–50 g (1½–2 oz) red pickled ginger
toasted sesame seeds, to garnish

Gyudon – a humble bowl of beef on rice – is kind of like the Japanese equivalent of a burger. It's fine for lunch, decent for dinner, but where it really shines is well into a night of heavy drinking. Sweet and beefy and savoury and satisfying (and almost impossibly cheap in Japan), it's something I could eat for just about every meal, just about every day.

METHOD

Place the beef in the freezer for about 30 minutes to firm up, then slice it against the grain into very thin strips.

Heat the oil in a large frying pan (skillet) and add the onions. Cook over a medium heat until they are soft and brown, then add the beef and ginger. Let the beef brown a bit, then add the sweet soy sauce and dashi and let it reduce slightly, to the consistency of a thin syrup.

Place the rice in deep bowls and spoon over the beef and onions along with the sauce, then garnish with the pickled ginger and sesame seeds. If this doesn't make you feel all warm and wonderful inside, you may be some kind of robot.

CHAHAN

FRIED RICE

SERVES 4

The first thing I ever learned to cook was macaroni and cheese (from a box, if you can call that cooking). The second thing I ever learned to cook was egg salad sandwiches (again, if you can call that cooking). And the third thing I ever learned to cook, if memory serves, was fried rice.

Fried rice is awesome on so many levels. First of all, it's easy. Like, really easy. Very little can go wrong in making fried rice. Also, it's satisfying and really full of flavour, *plus* it's a great use for leftovers – in fact, that's what I usually make it from. It's like my Japanese version of bubble and squeak, taking particularly well to finely sliced roast meats and veg. This is a sort of basic recipe for fried rice, but feel free to embellish it however you like. Delicious additions you may want to try include king prawns (shrimp), chicken, scallops, squid, Chinese chives, salmon and pork.

By the way, this works better with rice that has been in the fridge overnight. I frequently make more rice than I need just so I have an excuse to make fried rice the next day.

DIFFICULTY

So not difficult that I could cook this when I was a completely inept and awkward 14-year-old

- 1 tablespoon oil
- 4 rashers of smoked streaky bacon (dry-cured, if possible)
- 1 onion, finely diced
- 150 g (5 oz) shiitake (de-stemmed) or chestnut mushrooms, finely sliced
- 1 carrot, diced
- 4 eggs
- 4 garlic cloves, finely chopped
- 4 spring onions (scallions), roughly chopped
- 4 large portions of cooked rice (350–400 g/12–14 oz/ 1¾–2 cups uncooked)
- 3 tablespoons soy sauce
- 1 tablespoon sesame oil
- 1½ tablespoons mirin
- ¼ teaspoon dashi powder
- 50 g (2 oz) red pickled ginger
- 1 teaspoon toasted sesame seeds
- freshly ground black pepper
- handful of katsuobushi (optional)

METHOD

Heat the oil in a frying pan (skillet) or wok and add the bacon. Cook until golden brown and crisp, then remove and drain on kitchen paper (keep the bacon fat in the pan). Crumble or chop the bacon into small pieces.

Add the onion to the hot bacon fat and stir-fry until translucent and beginning to brown, then add the shiitake, carrot and eggs, and stir to break up and scramble the eggs. Add the garlic and spring onions and fry briefly, then add the rice, soy sauce, sesame oil, mirin and dashi powder. Break up the rice with a wooden spoon as you stir-fry, ensuring that there are no clumps. When the rice has absorbed all the liquid in the pan, add the pickled ginger, sesame seeds, some pepper and the bacon bits, and stir through. Serve in shallow bowls, topped with katsuobushi, if you like.

KINOKO TAKIKOMI GOHAN

JAPANESE-STYLE MUSHROOM PILAF

SERVES 2 AS A MAIN,
4 AS A SIDE

This one-pot Japanese pilaf-type dish, called *takikomi gohan*, is excellent as a side, but it can be a meal on its own as well. Comfort food at its umami-dense best.

METHOD

Place the rice in a saucepan with a snug-fitting lid and add the dashi, soy sauce, mirin and sake. Place the kombu on top of the rice, followed by the prepared vegetables. Set the pan over a high flame on a small burner and bring to the boil with the lid off. Place the lid on the pan, reduce the heat to as low as possible and steam for 15 minutes. Remove from the heat and gently fold the vegetables through the rice (discard the kombu). Serve topped with sesame seeds.

DIFFICULTY

Not difficult. At all.
It's even easy to
wash up after.

300 g (10½ oz/1½ cups) rice, washed
350 ml (12 fl oz/scant 1½ cups) dashi
1 tablespoon soy sauce
1 tablespoon mirin
1 tablespoon sake
small piece of kombu (6–8 cm/ 2½–3½ in), rinsed under cold water to soften
½ carrot, peeled and cut into thin batons
1 turnip, peeled and diced
200 g (7 oz) mushrooms – I like a mix of shiitake, oyster, and enoki (de-stemmed if necessary), thinly sliced
toasted sesame seeds, to garnish

SHICHIMENCHO KASHIWA MESHI

SOY-BRAISED TURKEY MINCE RICE

SERVES 4

DIFFICULTY

Ridiculously not difficult

This dish, a speciality of the city where I lived in Japan, is traditionally done with braised, shredded chicken. However, I find it's just as good (maybe better?) and definitely easier with turkey mince. Even if you don't like turkey you should give this a go: it's meaty and moreish and sweet and lovely. It is also surprisingly good cold, so leftovers make an excellent bento (lunch box).

- 4 eggs
- pinch of salt
- 2 tablespoons mirin
- about 2 tablespoons oil
- 2 garlic cloves, finely chopped
- 2 cm (¾ in) piece of fresh ginger, peeled and finely chopped
- 500 g (1 lb 2 oz) minced (ground) turkey
- 4 tablespoons soy sauce
- 1 tablespoon sake
- 1 tablespoon caster (superfine) or granulated (raw) sugar
- 1 tablespoon hot ginger beer (optional)
- pinch of dashi powder (optional)
- 1 teaspoon toasted sesame seeds, plus an extra pinch, to garnish
- 4 portions of cooked rice (300 g/10½ oz/ 1½ cups uncooked)
- 1 sheet of nori, finely shredded with scissors
- 50–60 g (2–2½ oz) red pickled ginger (optional)

METHOD

Beat the eggs, salt and 1 tablespoon of the mirin together.

Pour a little of the oil into a non-stick frying pan (skillet) and spread it around with a bit of kitchen paper. Place the pan over a high heat and pour in a little of the beaten egg, covering the pan in a very thin, crêpe-like layer. The egg should be thin enough to cook through from one side – if it isn't, pop it under the grill briefly until the top is no longer squidgy. Carefully remove the egg crêpe to a chopping board and repeat the process until all the egg is gone. Cut the egg crêpes into wide ribbons, then stack these up and julienne them as finely as you can – basically, we are making egg 'threads' that will go on top as a garnish.

Pour a little more oil in the pan and add the garlic and ginger. When it starts to sizzle, add the turkey mince and break it up. When the turkey is nicely browned and cooked through, add the soy sauce, sake, sugar, remaining tablespoon of mirin, and the ginger beer and dashi powder, if using.

Let the mixture cook until the liquid has reduced to a thick sauce, then stir through the sesame seeds. To serve, portion the rice out into shallow bowls and top with the turkey mince, egg threads and shredded nori, in three distinct stripes. Sprinkle the turkey mince with sesame seeds and place a little mound of pickled red ginger in the centre of the bowl.

KAIRUI NO DORIA

JAPANESE RICE GRATIN OF SHELLFISH

SERVES 4

DIFFICULTY

Perhaps difficult to understand how this dish is Japanese, but not difficult to make or devour

There is a subset of Japanese cuisine called *yoshoku*, which literally translates as 'Western food'. The thing is, it's not Western food as anyone in the actual 'West' would recognise. Instead, it's cooking that is unique to Japan, but with flavours and methods based in non-Japanese gastronomy. (I say 'non-Japanese' rather than 'Western' because even some dishes of Chinese and Indian origin fall into the yoshoku category in Japan.) This is the realm of okonomiyaki, katsu curry, *nikujaga*... quite a lot of the recipes in this book, actually!

One lesser-known dish in the pantheon of yoshoku is *doria*, a rice-based gratin invented by a Swiss chef working in Yokohama in the 1920s. It's actually a fairly standard gratin dish, but rice and a bit of miso give it a subtly Japanese edge. It is a distant cousin, flavour-wise, of Crab Cream Croquettes (page 67).

- 45 g (1¾ oz/3½ tablespoons) butter, plus extra for greasing
- 1 onion, finely diced
- 1 garlic clove, finely chopped
- 4½ tablespoons plain (all-purpose) flour
- 480 ml (16 fl oz/scant 2 cups) full-fat (whole) milk
- 100 ml (3½ fl oz/scant ½ cup) double (heavy) cream
- 3 tablespoons white wine
- 50 g (2 oz) miso
- pinch of ground nutmeg (optional)
- freshly ground black pepper
- 100 g (3½ oz) 50–50 mixture of white and dark crab meat
- 150–200 g (5–7 oz) king prawns (shrimp), peeled and deveined
- 150–200 g (5–7 oz) scallops
- bunch of chives, thinly sliced
- 50 g (2 oz) Parmesan or pecorino cheese, grated
- 50 g (2 oz) mature Cheddar cheese, grated
- 100 g (3½ oz) Gruyère, Emmental or Comté cheese, grated
- 40–50 g (1½–2 oz/1–1¼ cups) panko breadcrumbs
- 4 hot portions of cooked rice (300 g/10½ oz/ 1½ cups uncooked)

METHOD

Preheat the grill (broiler) to medium. Melt the butter in a saucepan and add the onion. Cook over a medium heat until soft and translucent, then add the garlic and cook until soft. Whisk in the flour to form a roux, then add the milk in a slow, steady stream while whisking constantly to prevent lumps from forming. Once the milk has all been incorporated, add the cream, wine, miso, nutmeg, if using, and pepper to taste, and whisk thoroughly to break up the miso. Bring to the boil, add the crab, prawns and scallops and cook for about 5 minutes until the shellfish are cooked through, then remove from the heat and stir in the chives, reserving a few to garnish.

Mix together the grated cheeses and panko. Grease a baking tin or flameproof casserole with butter and scoop the rice into an even layer on the bottom. Pour over the shellfish mixture, then cover with the cheese-panko mixture. Grill (broil) on medium until the surface is browned and bubbly. Garnish with the reserved chives.

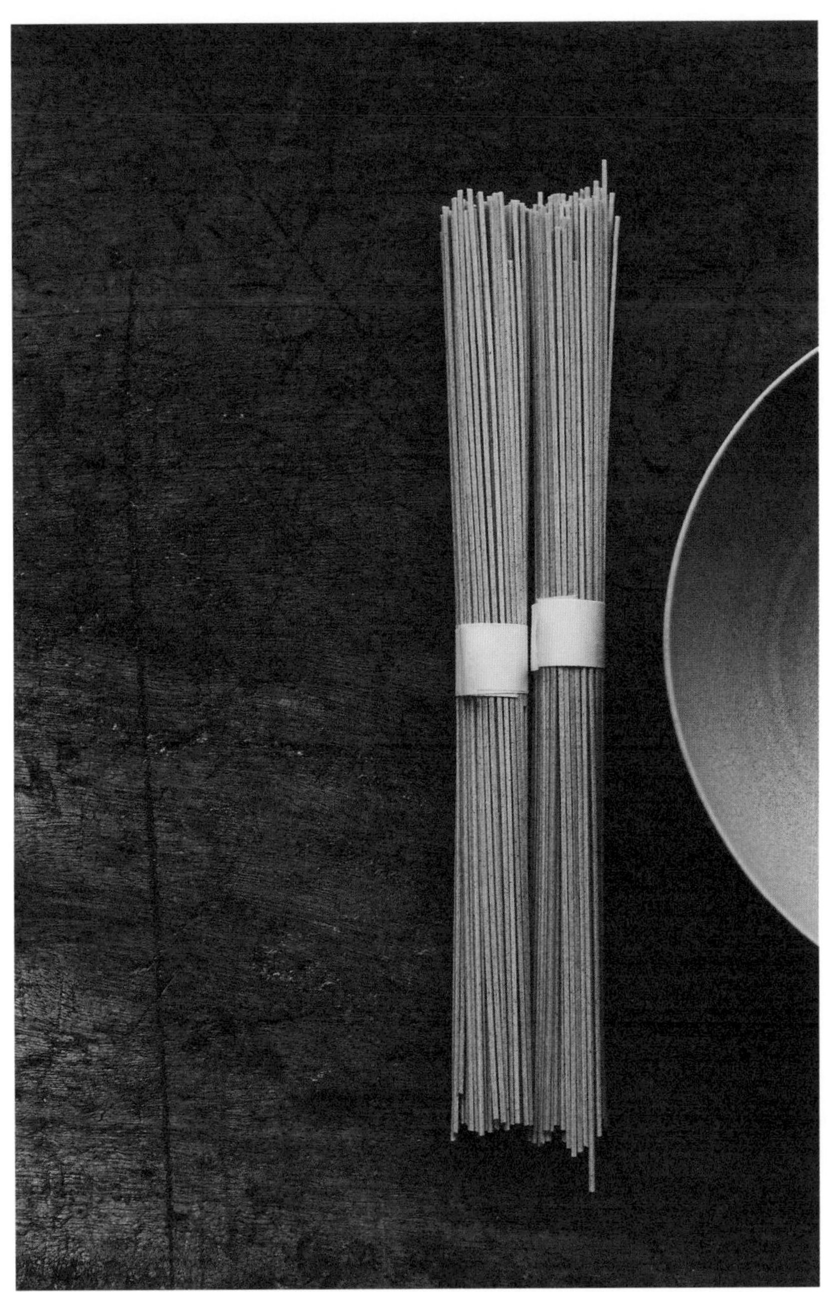

HOT UDON OR SOBA

SERVES 4

DIFFICULTY

Tremendously not difficult

1 block (300 g/10½ oz) of firm tofu
oil, for shallow-frying
1 litre (34 fl oz/4 cups) dashi
100 ml (3½ fl oz/scant ½ cup) mirin
80–120 ml (3–4 fl oz/⅓–½ cup) soy sauce, to taste
4 portions of udon or soba noodles
2 spring onions (scallions), finely sliced
toasted sesame seeds
4 eggs, poached or soft-boiled (optional)

Before ramen, there was udon and soba. I mean this in a historical sense as well as a personal one. Udon (thick wheat noodles) and soba (thin buckwheat noodles) predate ramen in the history of Japanese food, enjoyed as early as the 17th century, whereas ramen is a more recent invention, originating towards the end of the 19th century. The long history of udon and soba, combined with the fact that they are typically served in a very 'Japanese' dashi-based broth, may be why they are considered more traditional than ramen, which still retains some of its foreign cultural odour. (Ramen originated in China. But so did udon and soba – just longer ago.)

I also started slurping udon and soba before ramen. When I was first exploring Japanese food as a teenager, first in Milwaukee and then in Los Angeles, udon and soba were just more common. Practically every Japanese restaurant served them. Ramen was a slightly more niche thing. And although ramen became my one true noodle love (I fell head-over-trotters for my first bowl of properly rich *tonkotsu* pork broth ramen), I still have quite a lot of affection for the more delicate – but still satisfying – udon and soba. Ramen, for all its charms, can sometimes feel like a punch in the gut. Udon and soba feel more like a big hug.

This is a very basic recipe for udon and soba in hot broth, with just a few simple toppings. If you want to embellish your noodles a bit more, there are some suggested recipes in the pages that follow.

METHOD

Microwave the tofu on high for 2 minutes to express excess water (if you don't have a microwave, you can gently weigh the tofu down under a plate or two to gradually squeeze out the water – but this takes a good hour or so). Cut the tofu into thin slices, roughly 5 mm (¼ in) thick.

Pour oil into a wide, non-stick frying pan (skillet) to a depth of at least 5 mm (¼ in) and set over a high heat. Pat the tofu slices dry with kitchen paper and gently lay them in the hot oil. Cook on both sides until golden brown, then carefully remove them with a slotted spoon and drain on kitchen paper.

Pour the dashi, mirin and soy sauce into a saucepan and bring to a simmer. Taste and adjust the seasoning with soy sauce as you like.

Bring a large pot of water to a rolling boil and cook the noodles according to the package instructions. Soba should be simmered – anywhere between 5 and 10 minutes, so taste frequently. If you're using fresh udon, it will hardly need more than a minute. When the noodles are al dente, drain them and transfer to deep bowls. Pour over the broth and garnish with the fried tofu, spring onions, sesame seeds and eggs, if using.

KARE UDON

CURRY UDON

SERVES 4

DIFFICULTY

Supremely not difficult

Japanese curry and udon: a comfort food power couple. The addition of curry to hot udon doubles down on its warming, satisfying qualities – I love all kinds of udon, but this may be my favourite.

- 2 tablespoons vegetable oil
- 1 large onion, thinly sliced
- 1 green chilli, very finely chopped
- 2 garlic cloves, very finely chopped
- 1 red (bell) pepper, diced
- 60 g (2 oz/½ stick) butter
- 6 tablespoons plain (all-purpose) flour
- 45 g (1¾ oz) Madras curry powder (you can use hot or mild, or a combination of both)
- 2 tablespoons garam masala
- 1.2 litres (41 fl oz/5 cups) chicken or beef stock, dashi, or any combination of the three
- 4 tablespoons soy sauce, or more to taste
- 4 tablespoons ketchup or Tonkatsu Sauce (page 182)
- salt
- 1 sweetcorn cob, or 150 g (5 oz) tinned sweetcorn
- 4 portions of udon noodles
- 2 spring onions (scallions), finely sliced
- 4 eggs, poached or soft-boiled
- pinch of dried chilli flakes (optional)
- 40–50 g (1½–2 oz) red pickled ginger (optional)
- 50 g (2 oz) Cheddar cheese, grated (optional – but it's DELICIOUS)
- toasted sesame seeds

METHOD

Heat the oil in a saucepan over a medium heat and add the onion. Cook until lightly browned, then add the chilli, garlic and red pepper. Continue to cook until the garlic has softened and the pepper has started to brown.

Remove the veg from the pan with a slotted spoon and reserve. Add the butter to the pan and let it melt, then whisk in the flour. Cook until the roux turns a light golden brown, stirring constantly. Add the curry powder and garam masala, reduce the heat to low and cook for a few minutes, stirring frequently. Add the stock or dashi in a thin stream, whisking constantly to prevent lumps, and bring to the boil. Add the soy sauce and ketchup or tonkatsu sauce and reduce to a simmer.

If using a sweetcorn cob, blanch in boiling water then cut off the kernels, or heat up the tinned sweetcorn in a saucepan or the microwave.

Cook the udon according to the package instructions, then drain and portion into deep bowls. Pour over the curry broth and top with the sweetcorn kernels, sautéed onion and pepper mixture, spring onions, eggs, chilli flakes, pickled ginger, cheese, if using, and sesame seeds.

COLD UDON OR SOBA WITH HOT DIPPING SAUCE

SERVES 4

DIFFICULTY

Completely not difficult

In Japan udon and soba shops offer their noodles *hiya-atsu* – literally 'hot-cold'. The noodles are served cold, and the broth, highly concentrated, is served hot. This has a couple of key advantages: the noodles won't lose their texture if they sit in the broth for too long, and the temperature is naturally regulated so you don't risk scalding your mouth. At the end of the meal, the sauce is topped up with hot water to dilute it, and customers drink the resulting broth as a kind of warming digestif.

600 ml (20 fl oz/2½ cups) strong dashi (if you're making it from scratch, page 170, use Ichiban Dashi, or a double-strength brew of instant dashi)
120 ml (4 fl oz/scant ½ cup) mirin
150 ml (5 fl oz/⅔ cup) soy sauce
2 cm (¾ in) piece of fresh ginger, thinly sliced (no need to peel)
4 portions of udon or soba noodles
2 spring onions (scallions), finely sliced
½ sheet of nori, finely shredded with scissors
toasted sesame seeds

METHOD

Combine the dashi, mirin, soy sauce and ginger in a saucepan and bring to the boil. Hold at a simmer while you prepare the noodles.

Cook the noodles according to the package instructions (5–8 minutes at a simmer for soba, 1–5 minutes at a boil for udon), then drain and rinse them thoroughly under cold water. Massage and tousle them as you rinse, to get all the residual starch off. They should feel slippery and smooth rather than sticky and gluey. Drain them well, pressing gently to squeeze out excess water. Transfer to a plate or shallow bowl, and pour the hot broth into cups or small, deep bowls.

Garnish the noodles with the spring onions, nori and sesame seeds. To eat, grab a mouthful of noodles, swirl them in the sauce, and slurp. When all the noodles are gone, top up the remaining sauce with hot water and sip the broth, contentedly.

TOPPINGS FOR UDON AND SOBA

I love the minimalism of a basic bowl of udon or soba – just noodles and broth, perfect in their harmonious simplicity – but they do take well to toppings. On the next few pages are some ideas to add bulk and texture to your noodles, making them more of a proper dinner than a light lunch.

PAN-ROASTED DUCK BREAST

MAKES ENOUGH FOR 4 BOWLS OF NOODLES

Duck isn't a very common ingredient in Japanese cookery, but it turns up frequently atop steaming bowls of udon and soba. Its meaty-but-not-too-meaty flavour matches the broth very nicely indeed.

DIFFICULTY

Ducking not difficult

2 tablespoons oil
2 duck breasts, skin scored
2 tablespoons soy sauce
2 tablespoons sake
2 tablespoons mirin

METHOD

Preheat the oven to 180°C (350°F/Gas 4). Put the oil in a frying pan (skillet), ideally ovenproof, and lay the duck breasts skin-side down in the oil. Place the pan on a medium heat to slowly cook the skin; this will help fat and moisture render out so the skin is nice and golden and crisp. Cook for about 4–5 minutes on the skin side, until a rich golden brown, then turn the breasts over and continue to cook for another 4–5 minutes.

Depending on how big the duck breasts are, you may want to finish them in the oven – put the pan in the oven (if it's ovenproof, otherwise transfer to a baking tray) and cook for another 5–10 minutes. If you have a meat thermometer, use it – for nice pink duck, you're looking for an internal temperature of 55–57°C (131–135°F).

Meanwhile, combine the soy sauce, sake and mirin. Remove the pan from the oven and put back on the hob over a medium-high flame. Pour in the sauce and roll the duck through it to coat, letting the sauce reduce to a sticky glaze. Rest the duck for at least 5 minutes before slicing thinly.

STIR-FRIED CHICKEN THIGH

MAKES ENOUGH FOR 4 BOWLS OF NOODLES

Like duck, the meaty but not overpowering flavour of chicken thighs works beautifully with dashi. This is sort of a stir-fry, sort of a quick stew, and it's not just good on noodles. It's actually damn tasty just by itself, and it makes a mean rice bowl.

DIFFICULTY

Unspeakably not difficult

2 tablespoons vegetable oil
4 skinless, boneless chicken thighs, cut into small strips
2 cm (¾ in) piece of fresh ginger, peeled and julienned
pinch of freshly ground black pepper
2 tablespoons soy sauce
1 tablespoon mirin
1 tablespoon sake
1 tablespoon caster (superfine) sugar
toasted sesame seeds

METHOD

Heat the oil in a frying pan (skillet) or wok over a high heat. Add the chicken and ginger together and stir-fry for 7–8 minutes, until the chicken is cooked through. Add the pepper, soy sauce, mirin, sake, sugar and sesame seeds, and continue to cook until the liquid reduces to a sticky glaze.

KAKIAGE

TEMPURA FRITTERS

MAKES 8–10 FRITTERS

DIFFICULTY

Delightfully not difficult

These delectable crunch-parcels are one of the most popular toppings for udon and soba in Japan, and it's easy to understand why. They start off crunchy and sweet, and over time the batter absorbs the broth to make for fabulously juicy mouthfuls.

- 1 carrot, julienned
- 1 leek, julienned
- 75 g (2½ oz) sweetcorn
- 50 g (2 oz) green beans, cut into 3 cm (1¼ in) batons
- 100 g (3½ oz) squid, thinly sliced, or prawns (shrimp), roughly chopped (optional)
- 2 tablespoons plain (all-purpose) flour
- big pinch of salt
- 1 quantity Tempura Batter (page 100)
- oil, for deep- or shallow-frying

METHOD

Combine the carrot, leek, sweetcorn, beans and squid or prawns, if using, in a bowl with the flour and salt. Toss to coat, and set aside for about 20 minutes so that the salt softens the veg slightly.

Heat some oil in a deep frying pan (skillet) or wide saucepan – if you're shallow-frying, it should be over a medium-high heat; if you're deep-frying, the oil should be 180°C (350°F).

Pour a little tempura batter into the mixed vegetables – just enough to coat them. Toss them to evenly coat in the batter, then use a slotted spoon to scoop up the battered veg, allowing excess batter to drain thoroughly before frying – make sure you use the bare minimum of batter to hold the veg together. Use a spoon or chopsticks to gently push the veg off the slotted spoon into the oil, taking care to keep them together in roundish fritters.

Cook the fritters for 5–6 minutes, turning once during cooking, until golden brown. Drain on kitchen paper and set them half-submerged into your noodle broth.

YAKISOBA/YAKIUDON

SERVES 4

Yakisoba and yakiudon are both stir-fried noodle dishes; yakiudon uses udon, of course, but yakisoba, confusingly, does not use soba. This is because *soba* is an antiquated catch-all Japanese word for noodles, since for many centuries, soba was effectively the 'default' noodle. Yakisoba actually uses Chinese-style egg noodles or ramen; soba's brittle nature makes them unsuitable for stir-frying. Whether you go with egg noodles or udon is completely up to you – it all depends on preference.

DIFFICULTY

Not difficult to make and even less difficult to devour

2 tablespoons vegetable oil
4 rashers of streaky bacon, cut into small chunks, or 60 g (2 oz) lardons
2 onions, sliced about 5 mm (¼ in) thick
1 carrot, cut in half lengthways and then thinly sliced on the bias
¼ cabbage, cut into 1 cm (½ in) strips
300 g (10½ oz) bean sprouts
200 g (7 oz) shiitake mushrooms, de-stemmed and thinly sliced
1 tablespoon sesame oil
½ teaspoon dashi powder
1 teaspoon freshly ground black pepper
4 tablespoons soy sauce
4 tablespoons Tonkatsu Sauce (page 182) or Worcestershire sauce
2 tablespoons mirin
1 tablespoon sake
4 portions of cooked egg noodles, ramen or udon
40–50 g (1½–2 oz) red pickled ginger
toasted sesame seeds
1 sheet of nori, shredded with scissors
50 g (2 oz) crispy fried onions (optional)
60 g (2¼ oz) Japanese mayonnaise (optional)
small handful of katsuobushi (optional)

METHOD

Heat the vegetable oil in a wok or big frying pan (skillet) over a high heat, then add the bacon or lardons. Stir-fry until lightly browned, then add the onions and carrot. Fry for a few minutes, until the onions are beginning to colour, then add the cabbage, bean sprouts and mushrooms. Fry for another few minutes until the bean sprouts soften and shrink, then add the sesame oil, dashi powder, pepper, soy sauce, tonkatsu or Worcestershire sauce, mirin and sake.

Let the liquid reduce to a thin syrup, then add the noodles, ginger and sesame seeds. Cook for a few more minutes to let the noodles soak up the sauce, then portion into bowls and top with the nori, and the fried onions, mayo and katsuobushi, if using.

SURPRISINGLY AWESOME ONE-HOUR SPICY MISO RAMEN

SERVES 4

Good ramen is pretty simple to make at home, but *really* good ramen is almost impossibly difficult. Our 'basic' ramen at the restaurant is a complicated two-day process and the finished dish has eight different toppings, most of which are made in-house and involve quite a lot of labour in and of themselves. So even though ramen is my favourite food, I almost never make it at home, and when I do, it's pretty much always instant ramen from a packet gussied up with a few simple toppings.

But a few years ago, I was doing some consultancy for a new Japanese restaurant that wanted to make ramen, but didn't have the time or space to dedicate to producing large quantities of rich broth and lots of toppings. At first I thought: Bah! It can't be done. There are no shortcuts to great ramen. But then I recalled a ramen shop in Sapporo called Keyaki that I visited in back in 2007. They did something I had never seen before, which produced an immensely flavourful and deep ramen in a matter of minutes: they stir-fried a combination of miso, pork mince and other seasonings in a rocket-hot wok before combining it with their broth, which browned the meat and caramelised the miso until the mixture was nutty and rich. I decided to give something similar a go, and it worked *wonderfully*. So here it is: a truly excellent bowl of ramen that can be made from scratch in under an hour. This, to me, is as rare and exciting as a unicorn.

DIFFICULTY

Not at all difficult, especially considering ramen usually takes days to make

- 1.4 litres (47 fl oz/5½ cups) unseasoned chicken broth (not from a stock cube!)
- 100 g (3½ oz) miso
- 2 bok choi, cut into quarters
- 150 g (5 oz) bean sprouts
- 4 teaspoons sesame oil
- 4 portions of ramen noodles – dried is good; instant is better; fresh is best
- salt or soy sauce, to taste (optional)
- 50 g (2 oz) Parmesan cheese, grated (optional, but it's soooooo good)
- 4 Soy-Marinated Eggs (page 166), halved

For the spicy miso pork mince

- 1 leek, washed and trimmed
- 40 g (1½ oz) miso – use red or barley miso if you can get it
- 1 tomato
- ½ onion, roughly chopped
- 4 garlic cloves, peeled
- 1 fresh red chilli
- 2 teaspoons dried chilli flakes
- 2 cm (¾ in) piece of fresh ginger, finely sliced (no need to peel)
- ½ tablespoon toasted sesame seeds
- ¼ teaspoon freshly ground black pepper
- ½ teaspoon Szechuan pepper or ¼ teaspoon sansho (optional)
- 2 anchovy fillets in oil (optional)
- 250 g (9 oz) pork mince – not lean please!
- 2 tablespoons oil
- 50 g (2 oz/3½ tablespoons) butter

METHOD

Get a large pot of water on the boil and bring the chicken broth up to a simmer in another pan. Add the miso to the stock and whisk to dissolve.

Next: the spicy miso pork mince. Cut the leek in half, and roughly chop the greener half. Finely shred the whiter half of the leek, and soak in very cold water until needed.

Put the green half of the leek, the miso, tomato, onion, garlic, red chilli, chilli flakes, ginger, sesame seeds, pepper, Szechuan pepper or sansho and anchovies, if using, in a blender or food processor and blitz to a coarse paste. (If you don't have a food processor, you can grate or mince everything by hand, or use a mortar and pestle.) Work this mixture into the pork mince to make a delicious pork paste. Now here is the important part: you need an EXTREMELY HOT pan or wok. So get your best, most reliable pan on a high heat a good 5–10 minutes before you intend to cook. Add the oil to the pan and then add the pork mixture, stirring frequently until it turns a rich brown in colour. (Don't shake or lift the pan – keep it on the heat!) Once it's all browned nicely and cooked through (should be about 10 minutes), remove from the heat and stir in the butter. Keep warm until needed.

Blanch the bok choi in the boiling water for about a minute, just to tenderise slightly. It should still have some crunch. Remove with a slotted spoon or sieve, then blanch the bean sprouts for even less time: 20–30 seconds will do. Remove them as well, and dress with the sesame oil. Get your miso-chicken broth onto a rolling boil at this point.

Cook your noodles as per the package instructions – generally 2–3 minutes for instant, 4–5 minutes for dried, and certainly no more than 1 minute for fresh (you can use the same water you used to blanch the veg for this). Drain well. Ladle 300–350 ml (10–12 fl oz/1¼–1½ cups) of broth into deep bowls, then add the noodles and stir them through to loosen them. Pour over half the spicy miso pork mixture and stir that through as well. Taste the broth and adjust seasoning with salt or soy sauce, if needed. Top with the remaining pork mince, Parmesan, if using, drained shredded leek and marinated eggs. Enjoy piping hot, and don't forget to SLURP!

RAMEN WITH SCALLOPS, BACON AND EGGS

SERVES 4

DIFFICULTY

Much less difficult than coming up with another way of saying 'not difficult' this far into the book

This simple but spectacular ramen was inspired by the café at London's Billingsgate fish market, which serves one of my all-time favourite breakfast items: a scallop and bacon bap. Of course, scallops and bacon is a tried-and-true combo, but they're an extra special indulgence when you have them for breakfast. Which is when I recommend you have this light yet satisfying ramen – especially if you're hungover.

- 1 leek, white part only, finely shredded
- 8 rashers of streaky bacon
- 40 g (1½ oz/3 tablespoons) butter
- 4 big fat scallops or 12 little scallops
- splash of white wine or sake
- 1.2 litres (41 fl oz/5 cups) chicken or fish stock
- 1½ teaspoons mirin
- 2 teaspoons dashi powder (or more or less, to taste)
- salt
- 4 portions of ramen noodles
- 4 eggs, poached, soft-boiled or Soy-Marinated (page 166), halved
- 2 teaspoons chilli oil (or more or less, to taste) (optional)
- toasted sesame seeds
- 50 g (2 oz) pea shoots
- freshly ground black pepper

METHOD

Cover the shredded leek in very cold water. Cook the bacon in a frying pan (skillet) over a medium heat until brown and crisp. Drain on kitchen paper and add the butter to the pan. Add the scallops and cook for 2–3 minutes on each side (or 1 minute for little ones), until nicely browned, then remove from the pan. Add the white wine or sake to the pan and cook off the alcohol.

Scrape any bits off the bottom of the pan, then tip everything into a saucepan. Add the stock and mirin, and bring to the boil. Add the dashi powder and some salt, taste and adjust the seasoning as necessary. Slice the scallops horizontally into thirds (or leave whole if little), and roughly chop the crispy bacon.

Bring a separate saucepan full of water to a rolling boil and cook the ramen according to the package instructions. Pour or ladle the broth into deep bowls, drain the noodles well and place in the broth. Drain the shredded leek. Top the noodles with the eggs, shredded leek, chopped bacon, sliced scallops, chilli oil, if using, sesame seeds, pea shoots and some black pepper.

HIYASHI CHUKA

RAMEN SALAD WITH SESAME DRESSING

SERVES 4

DIFFICULTY

Sincerely
not difficult

I have a fairly problematic noodle addiction – in all honesty, it's hard for me to go more than a day or two without consuming some variety of noodle.

One problem with the need to consume noodles so frequently is that they're often accompanied by a rich broth or sauce – it's too filling. So when I need a noodle fix that won't weigh me down, a ramen salad such as this one is an excellent option. The dressing is creamy but not heavy, and it's full of crunchy veg. Just add the optional protein suggestions to make it a dinner rather than a lunch.

100 g (3½ oz) mixed leaves – try to get a mix of peppery/mild and crunchy/tender – I like pea shoots and rocket (arugula)
½ cucumber, julienned
100 g (3½ oz) cherry tomatoes, quartered
80 g (3 oz) radishes, thinly sliced
250 ml (8½ fl oz/1 cup) Sesame Sauce (page 183), thinned with a little water and salt or soy sauce
4 portions of ramen noodles, cooked al dente and rinsed under cold water
4 eggs, hard-boiled or Soy-Marinated (page 166), halved
4 slices of ham, or 2 cooked chicken breasts, or about 300–400 g (10½–14 oz) smoked or marinated tofu, sliced (optional)

METHOD

Toss the leaves, cucumber, tomatoes and radishes together. Mix the sesame sauce into the ramen and portion into wide bowls. Top with the salad, eggs and protein, if using.

AJITSUKE TAMAGO

SOY-MARINATED EGGS

MAKES 6 SMALL EGGS

These are sort of a bonus for your ramen dishes, but for me a bowl of ramen does not feel complete without them. Besides, they're very easy to make – and great just to snack on.

DIFFICULTY

Eggceedingly not difficult

6 small eggs, cold from the fridge
150 ml (5 fl oz/⅔ cup) soy sauce
50 ml (2 fl oz/scant ¼ cup) mirin

METHOD

Bring a pan of water to a rolling boil, add the eggs and boil for 6 minutes and 20 seconds exactly. This gives them a totally set white, and a yolk that ranges from firm on the outside, to fudgy towards the middle, and still liquid right in the centre. To me, they are perfect – however, this method is for small eggs. If yours are large, cook them for 6 minutes and 40 seconds. If you store your eggs at room temperature, cook them for about 20 seconds less.

Chill the eggs quickly in cold water, then peel them and soak them in a mixture of the soy sauce and mirin for as long as you can (if you haven't got much time, don't worry – they'll still pick up the seasoning in about half an hour).

BASIC SAUCES

定番の調味料

The techniques involved in most Japanese home cooking will not be foreign to you – it's fairly basic stuff like stir-frying, grilling or boiling. In many cases, it's not the method that makes a meal Japanese, it's the flavours. These are some go-to sauces and condiments that can be used to 'Japanify' everyday ingredients or dishes, so I recommend making big batches of them to have on hand whenever a Japanese craving strikes.

& CONDIMENTS

DASHI FROM SCRATCH

EACH RECIPE MAKES ABOUT 500 ML (17 FL OZ/2 CUPS)

Dashi is the life spring of Japanese cuisine – it is the essential Japanese flavour, at the heart of so many dishes. Now, I wholeheartedly endorse using dashi powder to make your dashi – it tastes good, it's easy, it's cheap, and it's not a cheat – unless you consider the overwhelming majority of Japanese home cooks to be cheaters. Which isn't fair! However, it's useful to know how to make dashi from scratch, and the results are undeniably lovely. It also isn't difficult in the slightest, although it may be hard to find (or hard to justify the cost of) katsuobushi, one of the key ingredients. If you do splurge on katsuobushi, I recommend following the instructions below to make *niban* ('number two') dashi as well, to get more dashi for your dollar. You can even use the spent katsuobushi a third time in home-made *furikake* (rice seasoning, page 184)! Niban dashi has a lighter flavour than *ichiban* ('number one') dashi, so it is best used in conjunction with ichiban dashi or in recipes where a strong dashi flavour isn't required. You can also stretch out your niban dashi with an equal quantity of the instant stuff, which gives you some of the nuance and aroma of real dashi along with the economy and ease of store-bought. It's win-win!

DIFFICULTY

Not at all difficult, but it might be tricky to get the katsuobushi. If it is, not to worry – that's what dashi powder is for

Ichiban Dashi

10 g (½ oz) kombu (about a 10 × 10 cm/4 × 4 in piece)
600 ml (20 fl oz/scant 2½ cups) water (if you're being really geeky about this, use soft bottled water like Volvic or Smart Water – it will provide a fuller flavour)
20 g (¾ oz) katsuobushi

Niban Dashi

Used kombu and katsuobushi from Ichiban Dashi (see above)
600 ml (20 fl oz/scant 2 ½ cups) water

METHOD

Ichiban Dashi: Rinse the kombu briefly under cold running water, then place it in a saucepan and pour in the water. Place the pan on a low flame – kombu releases its flavour most readily at a temperature range from cold to just below boiling point, so the more time you keep it in that range, the more flavourful your dashi will be. When the water barely begins to simmer, with just a few small bubbles breaking the surface, remove the kombu. Keeping the heat low, add the katsuobushi and simmer for about 5 minutes, then remove from the heat. Once the katsuobushi has sunk to the bottom of the pan, leave to infuse for about 15 minutes, then pass through a fine sieve; squeeze out the katsuobushi for maximum flavour!

Niban Dashi: You will need to be a little more aggressive with the heat to get more flavour from your spent kombu and katsuobushi. Place them in a saucepan with the fresh water and bring to the boil. Boil for about 10 minutes, then reduce to a simmer and cook for an additional 20 minutes. Turn off the heat and leave to infuse for 10–15 minutes, then pass through a fine sieve – and don't forget to squeeeeeeze that katsuobushi again. At this point it is perfectly fine to discard your kombu and katsuobushi, or save them for something else (but no more dashi at this point, sorry).

Keep your dashi in an airtight container in the fridge for up to a week, or freeze it in ice cube trays or small containers to use as needed over the course of several months.

SWEET SOY SAUCE

MAKES ABOUT 350 ML (12 FL OZ/SCANT 1½ CUPS)

DIFFICULTY

Not difficult

Variations of this recipe are common in all kinds of Japanese dishes, most commonly *teriyaki* and *kabayaki* – the former used for pretty much everything, and the latter used for grilled oily fish, especially eel. Whatever you call it, there's a reason it's so common: it's *delicious*. Sweet, salty and umami, it's just a nice, trashy, cheap thrill for human taste buds everywhere. Try it on: chicken, pork, beef, duck, turkey, salmon, trout, mackerel, tuna, sea bass, cod, swordfish, scallops, tofu, mushrooms, courgettes (zucchini), squash, eggs, or my absolute favourite: roasted carrots. Teriyaki carrots are stupid good!

200 ml (7 fl oz/scant 1 cup) soy sauce
200 ml (7 fl oz/scant 1 cup) mirin
100 ml (3½ fl oz/scant ½ cup) sake, water or dashi (this is mainly to take the edge off the soy sauce)
100 g (3½ oz/½ cup) dark brown sugar
4 garlic cloves, unpeeled and bashed (optional)
4 cm (1½ in) piece of fresh ginger, thinly sliced – don't bother peeling it (optional)
2–3 teaspoons cornflour (cornstarch), mixed to a slurry with 1 tablespoon cold water

METHOD

Combine all the ingredients except the cornflour slurry in a saucepan, and bring to the boil. Reduce the heat to a simmer and cook until the consistency of a thin syrup – it should reduce by about a quarter. Remove the garlic and the ginger, if using, then whisk in the cornflour slurry and boil briefly until nice and thick. Leave to cool, and keep in an airtight container in the fridge indefinitely.

SWEET MISO SAUCE

SMALL BATCH MAKES ABOUT 180 ML (6½ FL OZ/¾ CUP)
BIG BATCH MAKES ABOUT 540 ML (18 FL OZ/GENEROUS 2 CUPS)

This sauce, or minor variations thereof, is perhaps the most used weapon in my Japanese arsenal. Its main flavour is the all-around awesomeness of miso, rounded out with notes of sweetness and acidity. It is great on literally everything (try it on buttered toast, for real) as either a marinade or a sauce, but its flavour becomes deeper and sweeter as it caramelises, so I like it especially in foods that are grilled or baked – for example, it is a key component in classic grilled dishes like Sweet Miso-Glazed Aubergine and Sweet Miso-Grilled Cod (pages 52 and 107).

Generally speaking, you should use white miso for this if you're planning to use it on fish, tofu or lighter-flavoured vegetables, and you should use red miso if you're planning to use it on meat or meaty vegetables like aubergine (eggplant) or mushrooms. But really, both kinds will work pretty well on just about anything, so whatever miso you prefer will be absolutely fine for a very wide range of dishes.

METHOD

Stir all the ingredients together until the sugar has dissolved. This will keep in the fridge more or less indefinitely.

DIFFICULTY

As not difficult as
it is delicious, which is to say:
incredibly not difficult

Small batch
100 g (3½ oz) miso
2 tablespoons mirin
2 tablespoons caster (superfine) or granulated (raw) sugar
1 tablespoon water or sake
½ teaspoon vinegar

Big batch
300 g (10½ oz) miso
90 ml (6 tablespoons) mirin
60 g (2 oz/scant ⅓ cup) caster (superfine) sugar
3 tablespoons water or sake
1½ teaspoons vinegar

TSUYU

SMALL BATCH MAKES ABOUT 300 ML (10 FL OZ/1¼ CUPS)
BIG BATCH MAKES ABOUT 540 ML (18 FL OZ/GENEROUS 2 CUPS)

This classic dip tastes very Japanese indeed. And how could it not? Its main components are dashi and soy sauce, two of the most distinctively Japanese flavours there are. This is essential for tempura and noodles, but it's also a good thing to have on hand as a go-to umami seasoning for all kinds of Japanese dishes, from hotpots to simmered vegetables and fried rice.

DIFFICULTY

The opposite of difficult

Small batch
2–6 tablespoons soy sauce
2 tablespoons mirin
180 ml (6 fl oz/¾ cup) dashi

Big batch
60–180 ml (2–6 fl oz) soy sauce
4 tablespoons mirin
360 ml (12 fl oz/scant 1½ cups) dashi

METHOD

To make the dip, simply combine all the ingredients. The variations in the volume of soy sauce are all about what you're planning to do with this. If you're using it as a light dip, for things like tempura or grilled fish, go with less soy sauce. If you're using it as a concentrated seasoning or dip for noodles, go with more soy sauce. But really it's down to your taste – start with a little soy sauce and add more if you think it needs it. The tsuyu will keep for a couple of days in the fridge.

PONZU

SMALL BATCH MAKES ABOUT 90 ML (3 FL OZ/⅓ CUP)
BIG BATCH MAKES ABOUT 280 ML (9½ FL OZ/GENEROUS 1 CUP)

Ponzu is one of my favourite Japanese seasonings, combining the moreish umami of soy sauce with the fresh zing of citrus. It's great with fish, gyoza, tempura and all kinds of veg – and it's especially nice combined with butter, which rounds out the ponzu's acidity and gives it a touch of rich sweetness.

DIFFICULTY

Not-difficult-peasy lemon squeezy

Small batch
4 tablespoons soy sauce
1½ tablespoons lemon/lime juice (you can use either or a combination of both)
1 teaspoon caster (superfine) or granulated (raw) sugar
1 teaspoon vinegar

Big batch
200 ml (7 fl oz) soy sauce
4 tablespoons lemon/lime juice (you can use either, or a combination of both)
1½ tablespoons caster (superfine) or granulated (raw) sugar
1 tablespoon vinegar

METHOD

Combine all the ingredients and stir to dissolve the sugar. Keep in an airtight container in the fridge for up to 1 month.

RAMEN SHOP CHILLI OIL

MAKES ABOUT 300 ML
(10 FL OZ/1¼ CUPS)

DIFFICULTY

Not so difficult

Fans of ramen and gyoza (and dumplings generally) will be familiar with this common tabletop seasoning, which brings an addictive, lip-smacking heat and punchy aroma to a wide variety of Japanese soul food dishes.

- 300 ml (10 fl oz/1¼ cups) vegetable oil
- 6 garlic cloves, finely chopped
- 2 shallots or 1 banana shallot, finely chopped
- 30 g (1 oz) fresh ginger, peeled and finely chopped
- 4 star anise
- 20 g (¾ oz) hot red chilli flakes
- 1 tablespoon Szechuan pepper (optional)

METHOD

Combine the oil, garlic, shallots and ginger in a saucepan and set over a medium heat. When the vegetables start to sizzle, stir occasionally to keep them from catching at the bottom of the pan. When the veg start to brown, remove from the heat – everything should be golden, and the residual heat in the oil should take them over to a light bronze. Add the star anise, chilli flakes and Szechuan pepper, if using.

Leave to infuse, stirring occasionally, until the oil has cooled to room temperature – about an hour. Remove the star anise and pour everything else into a jar. This will keep in the cupboard for about 3 months before the flavour starts to fade and go stale – but I bet you'll get through it faster than that!

SHICHIMI TOGARASHI

SMALL BATCH MAKES ABOUT 125 G (4½ OZ/½ CUP)
BIG BATCH MAKES ABOUT 250 G (9 OZ/1 CUP)

Shichimi, or more formally shichimi togarashi (seven-flavour chilli) is one of my all-time favourite go-to spices whenever something needs a little kick. It's like an über-chilli powder; it's not just spicy, but also savoury, nutty and floral-aromatic. It's great on just about anything (try it on chocolate ice cream!), which is why it's so common on Japanese restaurant tabletops. Shichimi and soy sauce are like the Japanese salt and pepper – a superhero duo to rescue food from blandness. By the way, there's no standard recipe for shichimi, so feel free to experiment with both the ingredients and the quantities in this recipe (dried orange peel is an excellent addition if you can get it).

Make a small batch if you are planning to just use this as a table spice, or a big batch if you plan to use it in recipes like soups or spice rubs for meat and fish.

METHOD

Combine everything in a jar, screw the lid on, and SHAKE, SHAKE, SHAKE. Keep in the cupboard for up to 6 months, or until the aroma has faded.

DIFFICULTY

So not difficult

Small batch

4 tablespoons chilli powder (the variety and heat level depends on your preference, but I recommend something on the mild side – I love Korean chilli powder best of all)
2 tablespoons seaweed flakes
1 tablespoon Szechuan pepper, ground
2 teaspoons toasted sesame seeds
2 teaspoons ground ginger
2 teaspoons ground white pepper
2 teaspoons poppy seeds

Big batch

125 g (4½ oz) chilli powder
4 tablespoons seaweed flakes
2 tablespoons Szechuan pepper, ground
2 tablepoons toasted sesame seeds
1½ tablespoons ground ginger
1½ tablespoons white pepper
1½ tablespoons poppy seeds

TONKATSU SAUCE

MAKES ABOUT 600 ML
(20 FL OZ/2½ CUPS)

DIFFICULTY

Not difficult

Variations on this tangy-sweet, fruity-savoury, Worcestershire-like brown sauce – an essential flavour in dishes like okonomiyaki, *takoyaki*, tonkatsu and yakisoba – are incredibly common in casual modern Japanese cooking. I was running a cooking class a while ago in which I taught the students how to make this, and one of them said, upon tasting it, 'Oh! You taught us how to make brown sauce.' And so I did – tonkatsu sauce's flavour is remarkably British, sitting somewhere on the flavour spectrum between HP and Branston Pickle, but it has a few Japanese flourishes to enhance umami and sweetness. It also has a delightful affinity with mayonnaise.

By the way, there's no need to get too nerdy about this, but generally speaking this sauce should be made a little sweeter for okonomiyaki (more sugar), more acidic for tonkatsu (more vinegar/Worcestershire sauce), and thinner and more savoury for yakisoba (more soy sauce/ Worcestershire sauce).

- 200 ml (7 fl oz/scant 1 cup) Worcestershire sauce
- 4 tablespoons soy sauce
- 2 tablespoons mirin
- 2 tablespoons dark brown sugar
- 1½ tablespoons vinegar (malt or rice, or a mixture)
- ½ onion, finely chopped
- 8 dates or about 3 tablespoons raisins, chopped
- ½ Granny Smith apple, peeled and grated
- 1 teaspoon hot mustard (English, Chinese or Japanese)
- big pinch of garlic powder
- big pinch of white pepper
- 200 ml (7 fl oz/scant 1 cup) tomato ketchup

METHOD

Combine the Worcestershire sauce, soy sauce, mirin, brown sugar, vinegar, onion, dates or raisins, and apple in a small saucepan and bring to a simmer. Cook for about 10 minutes, until the onion and dates or raisins are very soft. Add the mustard, garlic powder, white pepper and ketchup, transfer to a blender, and purée until smooth (then pass through a sieve if you want it really smooth).

Keep in an airtight container in the fridge indefinitely. PRO TIP: This is the best possible condiment for a sausage or bacon bap.

SESAME SAUCE

MAKES ABOUT 470 ML
(16 FL OZ/SCANT 2 CUPS)

DIFFICULTY

Not at all difficult

This moreish, creamy, tangy sauce is delicious as a dressing for both salads and warm vegetables, and it's also brilliant as a dip for roast, fried, grilled or braised meats – if you're making hotpots like Sukiyaki (page 110) or Chanko Nabe (page 111) then have this sauce at the ready!

- 5 tablespoons toasted sesame seeds
- 5½ tablespoons tahini
- 4 tablespoons mirin
- 4 tablespoons vinegar
- 3 tablespoons sesame oil
- 3 tablespoons vegetable oil
- 3 tablespoons caster (superfine) or granulated (raw) sugar
- 2½ tablespoons soy sauce
- 1½ tablespoons hot mustard
- 1–2 pinches of garlic powder
- 1–2 pinches of white pepper
- 1–2 pinches of dashi powder (optional)
- water, as needed
- salt

METHOD

Grind the sesame seeds to a coarse powder with a mortar and pestle, food processor or spice grinder. Combine with all the other ingredients to form a creamy sauce. Add water if you're using it as a salad dressing or dip, plus salt to adjust the seasoning. Leave it thicker if you're using it as a sauce or glaze.

FURIKAKE

MAKES ENOUGH FOR ABOUT 30 BOWLS OF RICE

Even for those of us who love rice, sometimes it can get a little boring on its own. That's what furikake is for – a salty-sweet-savoury seasoning to sprinkle onto rice to liven it up a bit. In Japan, furikake comes in a huge range of flavours, but many of them are simple variants on a combination of sesame, seaweed and salt, which is really all you need to shake you out of your rice rut.

DIFFICULTY

Not difficult
in the slightest

- 20 g (¾ oz) spent katsuobushi from making dashi (page 170), squeezed dry (optional)
- 100 g (3½ oz/about ¾ cup) toasted sesame seeds
- 3 tablespoons sea salt, lightly crushed
- ½ tablespoon caster (superfine) or granulated (raw) sugar
- 2 sheets of nori, or 2 tablespoons dried wakame or similar dried seaweed flakes

METHOD

If you're using the katsuobushi, preheat the oven to 100°C (210°F/Gas ¼). Chop the katsuobushi up into small pieces and separate the flakes as best you can. Spread them out on a baking tray and put them in the oven for about 45 minutes, until they're totally dry, then remove and leave to cool.

Put the sesame seeds into a bowl and stir in the salt and sugar.

Snip the nori into very small shreds using scissors, or, if you're using wakame, crush it into fine flakes using a mortar and pestle, food processor or spice grinder. Stir the seaweed into the sesame mixture along with the cooled katsuobushi, if using. Keep in a jar in the cupboard for up to 3 months.

DESSERTS

7

デザート

Desserts aren't really a thing in traditional Japanese cuisine. Sweets are enjoyed sparingly, typically as a snack or something to nibble on with tea. But that's not to say that there aren't a lot of options to indulge your sweet tooth in Japan – cakes, pastries and sundaes, typically infused with Japanese ingredients or combined with traditional Japanese sweet dishes, are enormously popular. These are a few easy options for finishing off your meal with uniquely Japanese flavours.

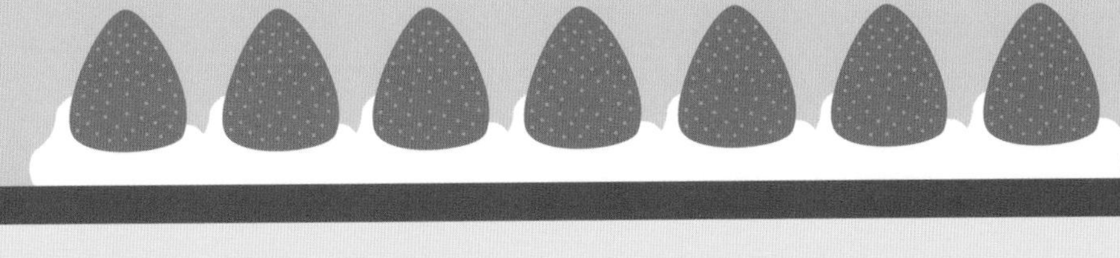

CASTELLA

MAKES 8–10 SLICES

Castella is one of the most popular sweets in Japan, introduced to the country by Portuguese merchants in 17th century Nagasaki. It is essentially a light sponge, typically enjoyed on its own with tea, but also as part of a dessert, often topped with ice cream, whipped cream and fresh fruit.

DIFFICULTY

Not at all difficult

4 eggs, separated
140 g (4½ oz/¾ cup) golden caster (superfine) sugar
2 tablespoons full-fat (whole) milk
2 tablespoons honey
30 g (1 oz/¼ stick) butter, melted, plus a little extra for greasing
1 tablespoon vanilla extract
finely grated zest of 1 orange
140 g (5 oz/1 cup) strong white (bread) flour
½ teaspoon baking powder

METHOD

Preheat the oven to 180°C (350°F/Gas 4). Using an electric mixer if you have one, whisk the egg whites until frothy, then gradually shake in the sugar, whisking constantly, until firm peaks form.

In a separate bowl, mix the egg yolks, milk, honey, melted butter, vanilla and orange zest together, then stir this into the meringue. Fold in the flour, a little bit at a time, until everything is smooth and well mixed.

Line a 450 g (1 lb) loaf tin with greaseproof paper lightly greased with butter. Pour the batter into the tin and shake it gently to level it out. Drop the tin a few times on the worktop to bang out air bubbles.

Bake for about 40 minutes, rotating the tin halfway through cooking. Remove and leave to cool for 5–10 minutes before tipping out, upside down, onto kitchen paper. Leave to cool completely before slicing into neat rectangles.

Serve with ice cream, whipped cream, fruit, miso butterscotch sauce (page 193) or brown sugar syrup (page 198).

MATCHA MASCARPONE POTS

SERVES 4–6

Matcha is the espresso of green tea – thick, intense, sharp and short. Its bitterness is invigorating for some, off-putting for others, but it's that intensity that makes it work so well in desserts – especially with sweet, creamy flavours like that of mascarpone or similar soft cheese. This is one of the easiest ways to enjoy matcha – even if you don't really enjoy it on its own.

METHOD

Whisk the milk and matcha together, breaking up lumps as best you can, until a thick, glossy, paint-like mixture forms. Add the vanilla and stir it through, then add the mascarpone, crème fraîche, sugar and salt.

Whisk until everything is smooth and incorporated, then keep whisking to thicken and aerate. You are essentially making a whipped cream using the fat in the cheese. Stop whisking when soft peaks form, then spoon into cups or glasses. Sprinkle a little matcha on top of each before serving.

DIFFICULTY

So not difficult you shouldn't have matcha'f a problem making this in under 15 minutes

2 tablespoons full-fat (whole) milk
1 tablespoon matcha, plus a little extra for dusting
1 tablespoon vanilla extract, or seeds from 1 vanilla pod
500 g (1 lb 2 oz/generous 2 cups) mascarpone, at room temperature
75 g (2½ oz) crème fraîche
100 g (3½ oz/½ cup) caster (superfine) sugar
tiny pinch of salt

MISO BUTTERSCOTCH BANANA SPLIT

SERVES 4

DIFFICULTY

So not difficult
it's bananas

One of the dumber purchases I've ever made was a refurbished dual-flavour soft-serve ice cream machine. Sounds fun, right? But it cost £2,300, weighed 150 kg (330 lb), had no warranty, frequently overheated, and just generally never worked quite right. I had it for about a year, until it basically stopped working entirely (it was churning my ice cream base into butter, not ice cream) and I had to get rid of it. Which eliminated our entire dessert offering at the restaurant. I had to come up with a new dessert menu quickly, and it had to consist of stuff that didn't require the oven (our oven is terrible, and early experiments with choux pastry mainly resulted in burnt, semi-inflated pancakes). This was the first recipe I came up with – it remains our best-selling dessert, I guess because it is just stupid good. And stupid easy.

- 100 g (3½ oz/½ cup) dark brown sugar
- 25 g (scant 1 oz/scant ¼ stick) butter
- 30 g (1 oz) miso (I like a dark miso for this recipe, but any will do)
- 1 tablespoon vanilla extract
- 200 ml (7 fl oz/scant 1 cup) double (heavy) cream
- 25 ml (1 fl oz/1 tablespoon plus 2 teaspoons) dark rum (optional)
- 4 bananas
- 8–12 scoops of ice cream (a few good flavours for this recipe: vanilla, butter pecan, salted caramel, pralines and cream, dulce de leche, Irish cream, and – the very best, if you can get it – cinnamon)
- 25 g (scant 1 oz) walnuts, roughly chopped
- 25 g (scant 1 oz) peanuts, roughly chopped

For the crispy noodles (optional)

- 1 portion of fresh ramen or egg noodles
- oil, for shallow-frying

METHOD

To make the miso butterscotch, melt the brown sugar and butter together in a deep saucepan over a medium heat. Whisk in the miso, breaking up lumps with the whisk, then add the vanilla and half the cream. Bring to a simmer, then remove from the heat.

To make the crispy noodles, heat about 1 cm (½ in) oil in a pan over a medium-high heat, then add the noodles, a few at a time. Cook until golden brown and crisp, remove with a slotted spoon and drain on kitchen paper.

Whisk the remaining cream together with the rum until soft peaks form. Assemble the sundae by splitting the bananas lengthways down the middle, then topping with the ice cream, walnuts, peanuts, miso butterscotch, rum cream and crispy fried noodles, if using.

DORAYAKI

SWEET AZUKI BEAN PANCAKE SANDWICHES

MAKES 6 DORAYAKI

DIFFICULTY

As not difficult as pie – actually, far more not difficult

Most Japanese homes and even restaurant kitchens don't have ovens – but that doesn't mean they can't have cake (and eat it, too). Home cooks in Japan have come up with clever ways of making cake in microwaves or rice cookers, but even without those methods they can still turn to this classic recipe for a sort-of cake fix. And they're much easier and taster to cook than an actual cake.

300 g (10½ oz) sweet red bean paste, or 200 g (7 oz/generous 1 cup) cooked azuki beans (tinned is fine) and 80–100 g (3–3½ oz/⅔–½ cup) golden caster (superfine) sugar, to taste
2 eggs
100 g (3½ oz/½ cup) golden caster (superfine) sugar
2½ tablespoons honey
1 tablespoon oil, plus extra for frying
½ teaspoon baking powder
150 g (5 oz/generous 1 cup) plain (all-purpose) flour
3½ tablespoons full-fat (whole) milk
½ teaspoon soy sauce (optional)

METHOD

If you're making your own red bean paste, drain the beans well and combine with the sugar and a splash of water in a saucepan. Cook over a medium-high heat, stirring frequently, until the water evaporates completely and the beans become very soft. Mash this mixture with a fork for chunky red bean paste, or blend in a food processor for smooth red bean paste (then pass through a sieve for super-smooth red bean paste). Leave to cool before using.

Beat together the eggs and sugar until the mixture becomes light and smooth. Add the honey and oil and mix well. Combine the baking powder and flour in a separate bowl. Add the dry mixture to the wet mixture a little at a time, stirring constantly to incorporate and break up lumps. Add the milk and the soy sauce, if using, and stir to combine.

Set a non-stick frying pan (skillet) or griddle over a medium-low heat (err on the side of low, because the honey and sugar in the batter have a tendency to burn) and add a little oil. Wipe the oil around the pan with kitchen paper – you just want a thin film of oil, not a pool. Use a small spoon or ladle to pour the batter into the pan to make small pancakes (ration the batter using a measuring jug if you are worried about running out), then cover the pan with a lid. Cook on one side until bubbles appear on the surface, then turn the pancakes over. Repeat until you have used all your batter to make 12 pancakes, then remove from the pan and leave to cool.

Once the pancakes are cool, spread a little red bean paste onto half of the pancakes, and top with another pancake. Enjoy with tea.

SATA ANDAGI

OKINAWA-STYLE DOUGHNUTS WITH BROWN SUGAR SYRUP

MAKES ABOUT 20 DOUGHNUTS

DIFFICULTY

Decidedly not difficult

In Okinawa these deep-fried balls of cake are called *sata andagi* – literally, 'fried sugar'. Which is a bit of a misnomer, because they're actually not that sweet. Not by themselves, anyway – but with a soak in traditional brown sugar syrup, or *kuromitsu*, they become an indulgently sticky and satisfying dessert (or breakfast – I'm not here to judge).

- 2 eggs
- 40 g (1½ oz/scant ½ cup) caster (superfine) sugar, plus extra for dusting
- 2 tablespoons honey
- 1 tablespoon butter, melted
- 1 teaspoon vanilla extract
- 200 g (7 oz/1½ cups) plain (all-purpose) flour
- ½ teaspoon baking powder
- oil, for deep-frying

For the brown sugar syrup

- 150 ml (5 fl oz/⅔ cup) water
- 250 g (9 oz/1¼ cups) dark muscovado or molasses sugar

METHOD

To make the brown sugar syrup, combine the water and dark sugar in a saucepan and bring to the boil, stirring to dissolve the sugar. Cool to room temperature before using.

Beat together the eggs and caster sugar until smooth and very light (definitely use an electric mixer if you have one), then whisk in the honey, melted butter and vanilla. Combine the flour and baking powder in a separate bowl, then add the dry ingredients to the wet ingredients a little at a time, stirring to combine.

Rest the batter in the fridge for about half an hour.

Pour enough oil into a very deep, wide saucepan or pot to come no higher than halfway up the sides, and heat to 160°C (320°F). Use a couple of spoons to portion out small balls of batter, dropping them (carefully) directly into the oil as you go. Fry for about 8–10 minutes, turning the doughnuts as necessary, until they are golden brown and cooked through (cut into one if you're not sure).

Drain on kitchen paper and roll in caster sugar while still warm. Serve with the brown sugar syrup on the side or drizzled all over.

DRINKS

8

飲み物

In Japan there is a saying: 'The foolish cat turns his nose up at sake in favour of tuna; the clever cat knows he can have both.' Actually, they don't say that in Japan, and I don't encourage you to offer your cat sake, but the point is, Japanese drinks are delicious and enhance Japanese meals beautifully, whether they are weekday suppers or special occasions.

EDO

A BEGINNER'S GUIDE TO BUYING AND DRINKING

S A K E

Fact:

SAKE IS LOVELY

Also a fact:

SAKE IS CONFUSING!

Many names. Many numbers. Many breweries. Many regions. Many styles. Many grades. Many methods. It's a lot to take in, and the truth is, even for people fairly experienced in buying and drinking sake, you don't always know what you're going to get by reading labels. But just a little bit of knowledge can help you find a sake you'll enjoy. (And even if you don't, hey, you can always cook with it!)

First of all, I have to get some bad news out of the way: really good sake *ain't cheap*. It's sad but true – there is not much truly delicious sake available in the UK for under £15 a bottle, due to import duties and the cost of shipping. But actually, sake preference is a personal thing, and if you like plonk sake, then by all means drink plonk sake! I happen to love a type of sake called Oni Koroshi, ('demon slayer'), which is so cheap and cheerful it comes in a paper carton, like fruit juice. It's also dry as hell, rough in a good way, and dangerously easy to drink.

So if you're just getting acquainted with sake, a good place to start is… anywhere and everywhere. I would recommend getting a bottle of **cheap stuff**, a bottle of **premium stuff** and a bottle of **oddball stuff** – I'll explain later. But first, some basics. Most sake rice is 'polished' before brewing, a process in which proteins and other compounds from the outside of the rice grain are rubbed off to expose the pure starch on the inside of the grain, which ferments more cleanly and yields a better flavour profile. This process determines the grade of sake, but there is another, overlapping categorisation based on whether or not distilled alcohol has been added, which also influences flavour, price and perceived quality. Alcohol is sometimes added simply to fortify and heighten aroma – so 'premium' sake may have added alcohol – but more often it's added simply to increase yields. Enter our old friend, the cheap stuff.

CHEAP STUFF

Cheap sake, or more flatteringly, table sake or 'normal sake', (*futsu-shu* in Japanese) is made from rice that's not been polished to any notable degree, and has quite a lot of added alcohol. It tends to be rougher around the edges with a pronounced alcoholic heat, and the use of unpolished rice yields strong, earthy flavours – expect notes of mushroom, sweet rice, malt and overripe/fermenting fruit. It is not usually very acidic, and it can range from kinda sweet to extremely dry. There's quite a lot of cheap sake that I enjoy, but buying them can be a bit of a crapshoot. Try a few (they're cheap, so you don't have much to lose) and if you discover one you like, then you're in luck! Make a note of the producer and try to seek out other sake from the same brewer or region. And if you don't find any cheap sake you like, no worries! Let's move on to the premium stuff.

PREMIUM STUFF

Premium sake, or 'special' sake, is defined by falling into any one of the following three categories:

JUNMAI

'pure rice': sake made from rice that has been polished to 70 per cent of its original weight and does not have any added alcohol

GINJO

sake made from rice that has been polished to 60 per cent of its original weight

DAIGINJO

sake made from rice that has been polished to 50 per cent of its original weight

Junmai is where you will generally start to notice a difference in aroma compared to table sake. With more pure starch exposed in the rice, and without any distilled alcohol, junmai tend to be smoother, fruitier, more floral, and a bit more delicate. *Ginjo* and *daiginjo* are often junmai as well, but sometimes they are made with a small amount of added alcohol. Either way, their flavours are super-refined and pretty much always extremely delicious and drinkable. They tend to be exuberantly fruity, with notes of pineapple and melon, white peach and even strawberries. They can also be floral, delicate and subtle. Even if you enjoy cheap sake, you should splurge on a nice junmai ginjo or daiginjo at least once – it is exquisite.

ODDBALL STUFF

In addition to the premium designations, there are a variety of other categories or descriptors to look out for when choosing sake, especially if you've tried a fair amount of 'basic' sake and are looking for new, unusual flavours.

- **Nigori:** Sake that has been very loosely filtered, leaving a large amount of rice sediment. It is milky white, often sweet and rich, and sometimes even a bit chunky.
- **Kimoto and yamahai:** Sake in which very old-school production methods are used to allow wild yeasts and bacteria to develop in the sake, producing funky, tart, earthy flavours. Think of these as like the sourdough of sake. They are some of my favourites.
- **Genshu:** Undiluted sake. Higher alcohol tends to boost aroma and make the sake feel more sharp on the palate, even if it's not very dry.
- **Taruzake:** Sake that has been matured in Japanese cedar casks. It has an evocative, rich, peppery, woodsy flavour that works well with rich and spicy food.
- **Koshu:** Aged sake. These are rare but often really, really delicious, calling to mind fine sherries.
- **Sparkling sake:** Sake with bubbles. These tend to be sweet and weak, and they aren't really my thing, but some people love them. Expect shandy-like refreshment rather than fine-wine complexity.

ON A SEA OF BLUE, THE WAVES FRAGRANT WITH LIQUOR, THE MOON IS A SAKE CUP.

MATSUO BASHO

Once you've chosen a few sake to try, get them in the fridge. **Almost all sake is best served chilled.** Rough, boozy aromas in cheap sake are less noticeable when it's properly cold, and the same principle allows delicate floral and fruity notes to come forward in premium sake – though some of these will be lovely at room temperature. I never really understood hot sake. To me, it makes sake taste too coarse and sweet – and like, you wouldn't heat up white wine, right? It's weird. But if you do want hot sake, it should be just a little warmer than body temperature, and DON'T YOU DARE use your nice junmai daiginjo!!! I'd recommend a junmai or smooth table sake to serve warm.

Lastly, sake is GREAT with food; I can't think of a time when I've tasted a truly bad pairing. But generally you should have cheaper, earthier, richer stuff with strongly flavoured dishes like curries, red meat or mature cheese, and pair more delicate, fruity, expensive stuff with lighter foods like fish, tempura or salads.

HITACHINO
ネストビー
JP
ネストビール

A FEW MORE JAPANESE DRINKS TO TRY

Not into sake? No problem.
Japan has a wide range of other options to go with your meal.

1 JAPANESE BEER

In Japan, beer is *the* drink, outpacing all other alcohol sales by a huge margin. I tried to find some hard data to back this up, but trust me – it's REALLY popular. And that makes sense, because beer is delicious! But also because Japanese beer tends to be light, dry, fizzy rice lagers. Their clean, bland flavour makes them easy to drink and food-friendly. My favourite is Kirin, but if I'm honest they're all pretty much interchangeable. These days you can also get a few different Japanese craft beers in the UK, which are really very good, and sometimes brewed with distinctively Japanese ingredients or flavours, such as sweet potatoes, yuzu and cedar wood. Definitely pick up a few bottles if you happen upon them.

2 SHOCHU

Shochu is a distilled spirit (liquor) that I often think of as sake's brusque redneck cousin. It's more potent than sake, at anywhere from 20 to 40 per cent alcohol, and can be distilled from pretty much anything, but most commonly rice, barley or sweet potatoes. It is sometimes described as a kind of Japanese vodka, but its flavour is far more complex and diverse. Just like sake, it can be earthy, nutty and rich, or light, fresh and fruity, and everything in between. If you're shochu-curious, I'd recommend getting one bottle of rice shochu and one bottle of sweet potato shochu, as they will deliver very different flavour profiles, so you can decide which you prefer.

3 UMESHU AND OTHER LIQUEURS

Umeshu is typically translated as 'plum wine', which isn't quite right. I would instead translate it as 'devilishly delicious sweet-but-not-too-sweet aromatic Japanese plum liqueur'. I don't really like fruity liqueurs, but I LOVE umeshu. Like sake, it comes in various grades of quality, but I actually think the cheapest of the cheap stuff is pretty tasty. It likes to be chilled way down, and served on the rocks or with soda (the latter is especially nice in the summertime). Similar products you may encounter can be made with other Japanese fruits such as yuzu or white peach, to varying degrees of deliciousness.

JAPANESE WHISKY

People have gone so crazy for Japanese whisky that it's actually become hard to get some of the more well-known brands (and if you do, it won't be cheap). But it *is* fabulous stuff. If you're going to go for Japanese whisky, I think you should *really* go for it – something that will cause your significant other to scold you for spending so much money. I'm a big fan of anything made by Suntory – and the older, the better. I once had a glass of 35-year-old Hibiki and it was so good it gave me goosebumps.

TEA

Japanese tea is delightful. It has a wholesome, grassy flavour that just feels refreshing and restorative when you drink it (of course it has nothing to do with caffeine). There are many, many kinds, but here are a few to look out for:

- **Ryokucha/sencha:** 'Ryokucha' just means green tea, and 'sencha' indicates that it is whole-leaf tea. Basically, these are catch-all terms for Japanese green tea and you will see both used on labels. There are a wide variety of sub-categories, but generally Japanese green tea is sharp, lemony, grassy and light. It likes to be infused around 75°C (167°F) for maximum umami and minimum bitterness.
- **Genmaicha:** This is green tea that has toasted brown rice added to it, giving it a rich, nutty, slightly sweet aroma and flavour.
- **Hojicha:** Tea that has been roasted until it develops a rich, caramelised flavour. Very comforting on a crappy day.
- **Matcha:** The espresso of green tea. Sold as a bright green powder, this thick and intense brew is not everyone's CUP OF TEA (sorry), but I find its sharp, fresh flavour makes for a thoroughly invigorating experience.

ABOUT THE AUTHOR

Tim Anderson is a MasterChef champion, executive chef-owner of the Japanese soul food restaurant Nanban in London, and author of *Nanban: Japanese Soul Food.* His affinity for Japanese food began when he first watched *Iron Chef* on TV as a geeky teenager – an affinity that developed into a full-on obsession when he moved to Los Angeles, and then Fukuoka, as a young man. He currently resides in Lewisham with his wonderful wife Laura and an FIV-positive cat named Baloo.

ARIGATO

Many, many people made this book possible. And not just possible – fun!

First of all, I must thank my wife Laura, who has given me her unwavering love and support throughout all my ridiculous (and risky) endeavors. Laura: I love you.

I must also thank my manager Holly Arnold, who has always represented me in the most sensible and sympathetic way imaginable. Holly: sorry I'm such a pain in the ass.

I also owe many tons of gratitude to everybody on the design and editorial side who did an amazing job of making this into the glorious and colourful book you have before you: our astute and fashionable publisher Kate Pollard; our meticulous and understanding editors Sally Somers, Hannah Roberts, and Kate Berens; our clever and quirky designer Evi O.; our gifted and efficient photographer Laura Edwards; and our most proper prop person Tabitha Hawkins. You are the DREAM TEAM!!!

Many thanks are also due to my colleagues and partners at Nanban, especially Pat Foster, Elly Foster, Rivaaj Maharaj, Suman Chaulagai, Krystian Myka, Ferdous Ahmed, Mark Robertson, and Anya Borgogelli, for their hard work and dedication to the cause of delicious Japanese food in Brixton and beyond.

Finally, I must thank everybody from whom I have learned the tricks of the Japanese food trade, whose tips and techniques and knowledge and know-how have been incorporated into my own repertoire and into this book: Emiko Pitman, Yuki Serikawa, Morgan Pitelka, Patrick Knill, Fumio Tanga and John Jones.

INDEX

D

E

F

G

H

I

J

K

L

M

N

O

P

Q

R

S

T

U

Y

Z

SAYO

NARA

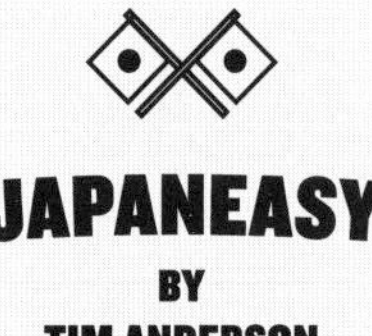

JAPANEASY

BY

TIM ANDERSON

First published in 2017 by Hardie Grant Books, an imprint of
Hardie Grant Publishing

Hardie Grant Books (UK)
52-54 Southwark Street
London SE1 1UN

Hardie Grant Books (Australia)
Ground Floor, Building 1
658 Church Street
Melbourne, VIC 3121

hardiegrantbooks.com

British Library Cataloguing-in-Publication Data.
A catalogue record for this book is available from the British Library.

ISBN: 978-1-78488-114-6

Publisher: Kate Pollard
Senior Editor: Kajal Mistry
Editorial Assistant: Hannah Roberts
Publishing Assistant: Eila Purvis
Photographer: Laura Edwards
Prop Stylist: Tabitha Hawkins
Art Direction: Evi O. / OetomoNew
Copy Editor: Sally Somers
Proofreader: Kate Berens
Indexer: Richard Rosenfeld
Colour Reproduction by p2d

Printed and bound in China by Leo Paper Group